AF600355

DRIED MILLET BREAKING

To Verlon and Angela Keema

DRIED MILLET BREAKING

Time, Words, and Song in the Wọi Epic of the Kpelle

RUTH M. STONE

INDIANA UNIVERSITY PRESS
Bloomington and Indianapolis

© 1988 by Ruth M. Stone

All rights reserved

No part of this book may be reproduced or utilized in any form or by any means, electronic or mechanical, including photocopying and recording, or by any information storage and retrieval system, without permission in writing from the publisher. The Association of American University Presses' Resolution on Permissions constitutes the only exception to this prohibition.

Manufactured in the United States of America

Library of Congress Cataloging-in-Publication Data

Stone, Ruth M.
Dried Millet Breaking

Bibliography: p.
Includes index.
1. Epic poetry, Kpelle—History and criticism.
I. Title.
PL8411.5.S76 1988 896'.34 86-46142
ISBN 0-253-31818-1

1 2 3 4 5 92 91 90 89 88

CONTENTS

Illustrations

Figures

Plates
(following page 80)

PREFACE

Into the silence. Only by the form, the pattern
Can words or music reach
The stillness . . .

T. S. Eliot
"Burnt Norton"

This study began from a puzzle. While working among the Kpelle people who live in central Liberia, I noted with some surprise text translations that appeared disjointed, disconnected, and fragmented. What should I make of a verse like

Sun falling, my friend Lanko Zoo-lang-kee.
Was that Wọi there?
What is doing that?
Let the song agree, let the song agree gently.
Wọi said, "That's fine." He said, "That's fine, then
I'm ready for the fight."

At the very moment I thought I was following a theme, a shift appeared and another topic was inserted. From that mystification, some fifteen years ago, I have been concerned with the problem of shifting themes in different areas of musical performance. I have studied the problem of musicians cuing one another. I have considered as well the drum patterns, horn hocketing, string ostinati, and call and response of bush clearing (Stone 1982, 1985, 1986). In this book I propose to follow the facets of timing as found in wọi-mẹni-pele, an epic that centers on the hero Wọi. I am concerned not only with the rhythms of music sound and the placement of music text, but also with the larger event flow and ultimately the movement of time for both the individual and the family, rhythms that impinge on those of musical performance.

The Wọi epic combines singing, narration, dramatic performance, and instrumental accompaniment to tell the story of the superhuman hero and his many adventures. The performance takes familiar elements and through magic makes them quite extraordinary. Wọi, for the Kpelle, is the epitome of brashness, bigness, boldness, and bravery and what he does encompasses in its course the sum of what Kpelle say life is all about. The Wọi epic expresses in a microcosm the imagination of several Kpelle generations of artists.

The book is organized according to themes that I interpret to be important for the Kpelle. These themes or patterns stand out in the foreground of what the Kpelle consider timing principles. Time, as I look at it throughout the study, is built by the performers of the epic and experienced by both the characters and the audience. Performance time, in turn, is enveloped by the time of everyday life in Kpelle experience. My nearly fifteen years of study of Kpelle expressive life have led me to identify a number of characteristics of Kpelle time, characteristics that I maintain are true of epic performance generally.

Time in Kpelle epic performance, as in other aesthetic expression, emphasizes qualitative elements. The epic singer relies on onomatopoeic language to suggest timing. Recent research in music notes the essential regard by African musicians for timbre in particular. Such attention stresses qualitative aspects rather than quantitative and chronometric aspects so often mentioned in Western ordering of time in music. Drummers memorize mnemonic phrases that represent the subtleties of timbre that they wish to produce, rather than a numerical sequence of ordering pitches.

The lack of quantitative emphasis does not, it should be noted, negate a complex level of synchronization. If African musicians don't stress counting, they are not thereby prevented from coordinating their movements. In fact, observers of African musical performance readily acknowledge that African rhythm is extremely intricate and complex. The result is achieved, for the most part, by synchronization that does not use a chronometrically based system of coordination. In other words, there is no clocklike basis for achieving the split-second timing.

In Western thought, quantitative time is often equated with precision. Thus Thomas O. Beidelman comments that the Kaguru lack our "precise" and "quantitative" ways of time-reckoning (1963:19). When we look at song and event time in African music, we see very precise timing evident with apparent absence of quantitative time reckoning. That Africans do not employ quantification in certain areas where Westerners do does not imply that they cannot or do not make use of quantification in other areas.

The absence of a clocklike mechanism for coordinating performance should not lead us to assume that Africans are incapable of reckoning time in a chronometric fashion. In Kpelle ritual performance, chronometric aspects assert an unusual importance not apparent in other types of performance. For example, while the exact occurrence of some musical event is often difficult to predict, the timing of certain ritual events is quantitative and entirely predictable. Upon the birth of a child, the mother and child emerge from the place of birth three days after the event if the baby is a girl and four days afterward if the baby is a boy. Likewise, after seclusion in Poro and Sande secret societies, young girls emerge three days after they enter the hut at the village edge and the boys emerge from seclusion after four days. Finally, the death feast occurs three days after death and burial if the deceased was a woman and four days after if the deceased was a man. Among the many examples that might be cited from other areas of Africa, in Yoruba Ifa divination poetry certain parts of the corpus are repeated a specified number of times (Abimbola 1971:38).

One sees in these particular cases an inversion of the normal predominance of qualitative time to emphasize the quantitative on certain ritual occasions. In the Kpelle case quantitative time is not associated with creative, progressive, or innovative elements. For the Kpelle it denotes re-creation and reproduction of the traditional aspects of life.

Some notable variations to the emphasis on the qualitative need to be pointed out. Somali poetic performance is based on very precise quantitative reckoning of syllables chosen and grouped according to implicit rules (Johnson 1982, personal communication). Certainly in other areas of life the skill of Africans with numbers is evident as well (Zaslavsky 1973).

Victor Turner's anaylsis of Mukanda initiation rituals in East Africa provides some parallels for the analysis here. In those rituals, distinct from "rituals of rebellion," Turner notes a preference for relationships which stress "likeness rather than interdependence." In a sense these relationships represent, when ritualized, the unity and continuity of the widest society, since they tend to represent the universal constants and differential of human society, age, sex, and somatic features. By emphasizing these in the sacred context of a great public ritual, the divisions and oppositions between corporate groups and the total social system, viewed as a configuration of groups comprised of all or any of the component groups, are "played down" and forced out of the center of ritual attention (Turner 1967:265). The ritual context then stresses unity and conformity, patterns of action different from those of everyday life.

Time in Kpelle epic expression, and in performance events in general, emphasizes the delineation of space. A music performance is special and different from ordinary activity in many African societies. The framing that is done serves to create a marked-off sphere and people may relate to one another differently than they do in everyday life. The quality of time felt by participants in the event may, correspondingly, be quite different from that of ordinary life. The special status accorded to events in many African societies has been noted as early as 1670 by John Ogilby, who describes a Sande girl's initiation closing celebration:

> When they enter the Town, or Village, there the People gather together as if it were some Holiday, the sogwhilly [head of the initiation ceremony] leads to the Sporting-place, where one sits Drumming with two Sticks on a round hollow piece of wood. By the ill-tun'd Musick of which (if so we may call it) Instrument,... everyone understands his time; and they all seek to exceed one another in Dancing. (1670:451)

As we look at time through the epic, we sense new qualities. An event, here defined as a bounded sphere of interaction (cf. Bauman 1977:27), frequently combines a complex of instrumental playing, singing, speaking, dancing, dramatization, and visual display, as well as a variety of integrally associated arts. The sound analysis that has been the central focus of scholars exists in a nexus of activity. Gregory Bateson has argued that grace is a problem of integration of the multiple levels of the mind, of both the "conscious" and the "unconscious" parts. Music writ large within an event demands a similar kind of integration. Our viewing of the event and its action requires a dynamic linking of multiple facets (1972:129).

Kpelle performance places considerable stress on qualitatively distinguishing music by reference to space. Actions occur in three-dimensional space and sounds occur "under," "above," "outside," and "inside." In epic events, heroes characteristically move in multiple planes and spaces, ranging from under the river to high in the sky. Thus, music in time assumes for the Kpelle a volume that contrasts to some Western notions of a more flat and linear progression.

This emphasis on three-dimensional, spatial aspects of musical time should not be equated with timelessness. On the contrary, evidence shows that this spatially delineated time is nevertheless a special kind of time that is motion filled.

Time in epic and in the wider universe of Kpelle expression emphasizes the concept of motion. Dancing, drumming, and singing all create in Kpelle thinking aesthetic principles of motion. Even in the epic text, Wọi's house moves to battle, the blacksmith's bellows pump, the woman's adze carves a bowl.

African accounts of performance in general also provide ample evidence of the emphasis on movement and motion. Even in the Afro-American context the motion metaphor is strong. Motion figures in artist Henry Dorsey's "placing of tractor wheels at certain corners of his house and along the edges of his property" to convey the image that the "earth itself was wheeled, could be mentally set in motion," in James Hampton's attaching wings to the main parts of *The Throne of the Third Heaven,* and in the use of train sounds by black musicians (Thompson 1983:156-58). A static state is by no means implied by the lack of linear progression.

The past, in epic, is dynamically manipulated in the present. While the most is made of the present and although music performances center on the present, the past is an equally essential element. The past provides authority and sanction for the present and is constantly referred to in order to create the present moment. The past enters into the present in a most active and instrumental way, however. The present situation is a context for adjusting and reproducing the past to best fit with the present action. Robin Horton's characterization of African thought as a "closed predicament" acknowledges the importance of the past, but it plays down the creative possibilities for manipulating that realm of experience (Horton 1967:177). Performers incorporate departed ancestors and deceased great musicians in the music event in an attempt to solicit actions favorable to the performance, particularly aid in improving their own playing or singing. Relationships of these departed are manipulated within the context of the present situation. Texts recall past utterances and knowledge, but are never simply repeated. As created anew in the present these texts are then viewed and experienced in light of the present situation.

It would be a mistake, however, to consider that in such acts the Kpelle are simply repeating what has occurred in the past. By viewing all interaction and performance through Giddens's concept of "structuration," we can recognize that change is inherent, even if not realized, in every situation of social reproduction (1979:210). The traditional is that which is authorized rather than that which is never changing, for the authorized is subject to alteration within the context of present performance activity.

The notion of historical past is particularly interesting. I will not argue, as Bonnie J. Barthold does, that pre-European Africa is characterized by a cyclic time, which later erodes into a period of temporal chaos, followed by a development of linear time (1981:6-7). Such an argument, with its undercurrents of cultural evolutionism, does not accurately describe the evidence presently available.

Barthold's characterization of African time as cyclic is, of course, a widely accepted generalization. This idea leads, as well, to the assumption that where there is cyclic time there is no change. And going even one step further one can reason that where there is no change there is also no time (Giddens 1979:198). Thus, African music is performed, according to some writers, in a kind of timelessness.[1] Such conclusions do little to illuminate the African and, particularly, the Kpelle perception of time.

Time in epic is contingent. Those elements which are part of the singer's repertoire do not include the entire composition waiting to be reproduced like a score stored in the mind of the singer. Rather, the singer's stock of knowledge incorporates phrases, patterns, and proverbs to be woven and juxtaposed in light of the performance event's momentary exigencies. The knowledge of process is crucial for the ethnomusicologist. Unpredictable actions by participants may create an event that proceeds in a number of possible directions.

Time in the epic is multidimensional. From an analyst's perspective, we can use several of Alfred Schutz's ideas to study time as created in the Kpelle epic. As a phenomenological sociologist and amateur musician, Schutz explained that music—and he was referring to Western music—moves in a series of coordinated dimensions. Some of these dimensions are of "outer time," of those chronometric types that serve primarily to coordinate the individuals making and experiencing music together. The conductor beating his baton is moving in this dimension. A metronome outlines the beats of outer time. Other time dimensions are from "inner time," the subjectively experienced qualitative time. When we find two periods of time measured as equal by the clock to be quite different because of our quality of experience, we are referring to this inner time. Though Schutz's conclusions are derived from Western examples, the essential point is that musical time cannot be reduced to a single dimension. Musical

1. Evidence is abundant throughout Africa that musicians can and do learn the Western conceptualizations when they are trained in Western art music, for example. It might be fruitful to consider that the ways of temporal conceptualization are based on capacities inherent in all humans but only selectively developed. Thus, some people may prefer linear progression of time as a way of conceptualization, others may select qualitative differentiation of timbre.

time appears to be the coordination of a number of simultaneously experienced dimensions. The nature of these multiple dimensions in various African societies remains to be researched and described.

The data from the Kpelle show that musicians shift rapidly from the outer time of keeping together to various kinds of inner time. For the Kpelle, however, outer time is not always quantitative. Furthermore, both outer and inner time can be qualitative time of different sorts.

Time exists only as a participant, a performer or an audience member, experiences it. Time is lived by people. Centrally, their interpretation of that time must be regarded in seeking to understand musical time. And since people live through time together, time flux is partially shared and, to the extent that it is shared, a vital synchrony between people results.

While we might, quite easily, accept this conclusion, we must consider how different it is from our commonsense notion of time as a unilinear entity. We have long thought of a musical composition as being created in a time that moves single-mindedly forward, measured, divided, and ordered by quantitative time; upon reflection we might accept that such is not necessarily the case.

For some years, ethnomusicologists interpreted African music from a limited view. Although they, unlike many music theorists and musicologists, may not have studied pitch more carefully than they did rhythm in Africa, they often began their search from certain basic Western assumptions. Most fundamentally, they often assumed equally spaced underlying beats (Waterman 1952; Merriam 1977; Jones 1959). While such studies usefully showed that order and, indeed, complexity of rhythm are evident in African performance, there are some important and subtle differences in the way Africans conceptualize these things. More recent studies, by Gerhard Kubik, James Koetting, Paul Berliner, and Roderic Knight, among others, have explored indigenous notions of timing and rhythm. Indeed, as Lewis Rowell has suggested (1986:5), our growing understanding of how Africans understand the temporal in music may lead us to ask whether there is not something new to learn about ourselves when we hold their ideas to our own practice of Western music, a practice little studied with ethnographic methods.

The Kpelle have been quite thoroughly studied by anthropologists and other social scientists. James Gibbs provides a good overall characterization in his essay "The Kpelle of Liberia" in *People of Africa* (1965). In addition, Kpelle folklore has been examined by William Murphy (1976), Kpelle women's lives have been studied by Caroline Bledsoe (1980), and Kpelle cognitive patterns have been tested by John Gay and Michael Cole (1967).

Though my study of timing in epic performance began in 1970, when I spent the summer surveying musical performance genres throughout Bong County in central Liberia and discovered that epic existed, the background for my work was developed many years earlier. A great part of my broad impression of the Kpelle stems from my childhood in Liberia, when I spent afternoons playing in the rice fields while Kpelle friends labored, or splashing in the local creeks where women fished. During that period I learned much of what I know about the Kpelle, including their language, without conscious effort.

After my initial musical survey in 1970 (Stone and Stone 1972), I returned to Liberia in 1975 and for fourteen months studied two performing groups intensively (Stone 1982). During this time, while my husband and I lived in Totota, I also recorded the epic performances to which I refer. There was much in the epic data, however, that I did not have a chance to follow at that time. Only in 1982-83 was I able to work through the earlier performances and conduct feedback interviews of the type that I had earlier conducted on cuing in music (Stone and Stone 1981). My epic text comes from a single area and a single storyteller, although my interviews refer to neighboring traditions as well. I present it here as an example of a tradition which is still widespread, if sporadic, and as an illustration of patterns that are sometimes found in other performances as well. My aim is to pull apart one moment of performance, extended though it may be, and use it to explain some salient temporal concepts of the Kpelle.

The Kpelle of Bong County participate in both an urban and a rural existence. The rice farmers travel frequently to weekly markets like those at Totota, Sanoyea, or Yanekwele to get cash for produce that is then whisked down the main highway to consumers in Monrovia. Some men live away from home for periods of time to work in the nearby rubber and iron-mining concessions. Others have moved their families to the concession towns, where houses with uniform exteriors have been placed in straight rows.

The Kpelle, living in villages reached by footpaths or auto roads, travel and move about a great deal. Some walk an hour or more each day to their outlying farms. Many frequent nearby or even distant towns where relatives and friends reside. Some men work in the capital, Monrovia, some ninety miles away and return at month's end to their families and homes and to special musical performances.

A pervasive force in ritual and everyday life is the men's secret Poro society and its counterpart, the Sande society, for women. Societies to which all adult Kpelle belong, these organizations not only help to socialize children, they provide the enforcement of hierarchy in social structure. They provide a source of authority not to be openly questioned. As the Quran is considered to be at the core of Muslim life, Poro (to be understood as including Sande) forms the core of Kpelle life. Poro shapes life through both ritual and ordinary action. The deep-seated temporal notions of Poro are continuous and changeless.

Kpelle aesthetic performances feature singing, dancing, playing of musical instruments, and speaking. These group activities require people to listen and to judge actively as well as to perform. Known as *pele,* these events are vital to emotional life for the Kpelle. The temporal ideas of these events are characterized by segmentation and continual change, in contrast to those associated with Poro.

This work will explore Kpelle ideas of time, which center on a complex mosaic arrangement. The Kpelle pattern is fundamentally different from the more linear ways of organizing performance that dominate Western culture. This Kpelle pattern influences how people think about performing as well as how they listen to and watch artistic performances. Sound pieces and patterns vary not so much by sequence as by juxtaposition. The Kpelle might be better pictured as sculptors than as stringers of sound-action.

ACKNOWLEDGMENTS

The development of this work has been facilitated by a number of events. A valuable period of library research in the summer of 1980 was made possible by a Summer Faculty Fellowship from Indiana University. In the spring of 1981, I organized, with two other colleagues, John Johnson and Ronald Smith, the Seminar in Contemporary Africa at Indiana University. The topic for that semester, "African Dimensions of Time," was addressed by scholars in the African humanities who spoke from their particular specialities: folklore, music, anthropology, and philosophy. The writing of the manuscript was made possible by a National Endowment for the Humanities Fellowship in 1982–83. During that time I was able to return to Liberia and conduct research among the Kpelle of central Liberia, following up the recordings of Kulung that I had made six years earlier.

I owe much to others who have contributed to this book. First, I acknowledge the great debt to the late Kulung whose renditions of the Wọi epic are the soul of this study. I am only sorry that he is not alive today to see part of his performance in print for a wider audience. Since epic performance is very much a group effort, I need to thank too those performers from Gbeyilataa who became the chorus, instrumentalists, and questioners. A number of them, along with John Manawu, John Woni, and Yakpalo Dong, also helped with long interview sessions in 1982–83.

My colleagues at Indiana University have been instrumental in helping me work through the ideas presented here. The late Alan P. Merriam engaged in discussions of African rhythms and his questions showed me new sides of the problem. Ronald Smith and John Johnson shared my enthusiasm to conduct a seminar on the broad topic of time in Africa. Lewis Rowell has shared my interest of time in music and has been a source of contacts, particularly in the world of music theorists. More indirectly my other colleagues in ethnomusicology have provided that ever-present and ever-necessary sounding board. To Mellonee Burnim, Portia Maultsby, Anthony Seeger, and Louise Spear I am grateful. Finally, Patrick O'Meara has given his clear support of the study of the arts in African societies in his capacity as director of the African Studies Program.

A number of my fellow scholars in ethnomusicology have assisted and stimulated my work. Among them are Dorothy S. Lee, J. H. Kwabena Nketia, Roderic Knight, Gerhard Kubik, Hewitt Pantaleoni, John Blacking, Sue Carole De Vale, and the late James Koetting.

A real pleasure of my work at Indiana University has been the climate of inquiry fostered by the graduate students with whom I work. I am particularly grateful to a number of them for comments that have caused me to look at things a bit differently: Daniel Avorgbedor, Jane Cowan, Sally Childs-Helton, Yilderay Erdener, Cornelia Fales, Laura Harris, Michael Largey, and Laurie Sommers.

A special thanks goes to Lydia Spehr, my mother, for checking important details.

More than anyone my husband, Verlon, has shared in this work. As photographer, audio engineer, and technical expert he was vital to the fieldwork team. During the past four years, when our careers often situated us half a world apart, he always upheld the place of this work. It is to him and my daughter, Angela, that I dedicate this book.

All the ideas presented here have been placed here through my interpretation of what I have read and been told. They need to be read with that understanding in mind. I also had the good fortune to write much of this book in Saudi Arabia and that country provided a fine contrast in setting that has served to sharpen my impressions of the Kpelle data.

MUSIC TRANSCRIPTION SYMBOLS AND KPELLE ORTHOGRAPHY

MUSIC TRANSCRIPTION SYMBOLS

♩̣⁺ sharp pitch but less than a semitone

♩̣⁻ flat pitch but less than a semitone

𝄠 sounds an octave lower

KPELLE ORTHOGRAPHY

ọ = "AW" as in awful
ẹ = "EH" as in bet
ɣ = "CH" as in the German ach
ŋ̣ = "NG" as in sing
ɓ = implosive "b"

DRIED MILLET BREAKING

CHAPTER 1

Battles That Never End

> The head of an epic does not comes out,
> You just keep bouncing.
>
> Epic singer

The wọi-mẹni-pele, which the Kpelle people celebrate, is about the superhuman hero Wọi. I came to know this epic through Kulung, the singer, storyteller, and conductor of the performances I attended. As one who could "pour out" this event, he arrived periodically in Gbeyilataa and stayed for several days at a time to spin his epic and to amuse the local residents. The ensemble I was studying became his chorus and he, if but for a short time, the featured performer. Thus it was through another project that I found this large and encompassing performance.

Kulung was one of only a few people in the Kpelle area in Bong County, Liberia, who could sing the Wọi epic. The young, interested in Nairobi rhythms and the sounds of electric guitars, found the learning of such a complex form beyond their inclinations. Though this music and dance—a form representing so much of the past—is in no immediate danger of disappearing, it is becoming a less well known, though still valued event.

Wọi-mẹni-pele, "Wọi's-matter-play," features a central character, Wọi. As a superhuman ritual specialist, a Kpelle person first among all other Kpelle, Wọi becomes the pivotal personage lacing the episodes together. His actions build what the Kpelle think of as embodying, and potentially capable of portraying, everything that is essentially Kpelle. "If one knows Wọi epic, one knows Kpelle life," many people say.

In a society ruled by numerous parallel paramount chiefs and lacking a central king or chief, this dominant hero is an interesting character. He is certainly not a mirror of the present political structure and is in many respects the complete opposite of what exists. He does, however, reflect something of the central rulers known in the savannah areas from where the Kpelle are believed to have migrated. And his wanderings from battle to battle may symbolize the movement from skirmish to skirmish for the Kpelle as they moved slowly toward the coast.

Like their Mande neighbors, the Kpelle possess an epic tradition, albeit one that has unique characteristics as well. The epic, in John Johnson's terms (1980:312), is primarily poetic, narrative, heroic, and legendary. Secondarily the epic is long, multifunctional, multigeneric, and a means to transmit traditions. The Wọi epic, as will become increasingly evident, is all of these. As poetry it exudes constraints of rhythm and timbre that are not found in ordinary speech. As narrative it unfolds a story of a hero that is taken to be true by the Kpelle. In addition, we can say that it is long, multifunctional, transmits traditions, and is multigeneric. Thus, the Wọi epic satisfies both the primary and the secondary characteristics described by Johnson. Beyond that, this kind of epic also contains sections of prose, music performance, and dramatic gesture.

PERFORMING EPIC

The epic event unfolds in one of the open verandas built at the front of village homes. The families have returned from outlying fields, the evening meal is over, and people see by firelight or kerosene lamps. Teenagers, middle-aged adults, old people, and children gather as a woven raffia mat is laid for the storyteller-singer. Like the Southeast Asian dalang or puppeteer, the epic singer serves as the conductor of the entire event. He keeps himself aware of all that is happening and communicates the need for adjustments to the musicians.

In the center of the gathering, the epic singer kneels to position himself on the mat. Near him he appoints two instrumentalists, each to hit a beer bottle with the back edge of a penknife and make the sound, if not the appearance, of the more ancient struck iron idiophone. The short, ever-repeating patterns they play interlock and, in their tinkling, high pitch, help create the warp of the performance fabric. This instrumental background (see fig. 1) is the fastest gait of the various parts in the performance.

Figure 1. Instrumental Background, Episode 1

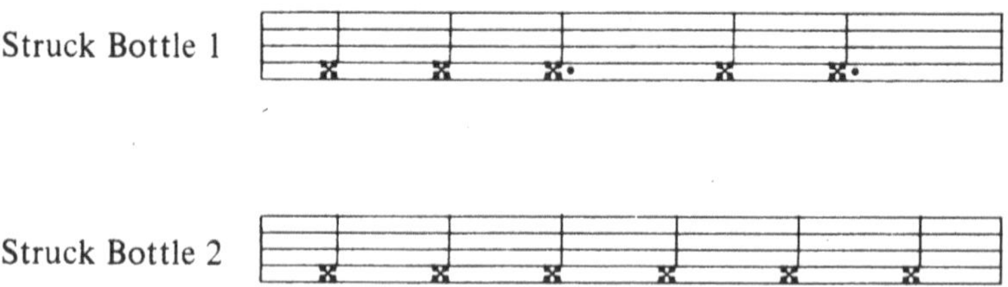

A chorus (see fig. 2) composed of audience members sings in the background continuously. Slower in pace and lower in pitch than the instruments, it forms a sound layer of distinct character. The short, legato phrases repeat without variation and interlock not only with each other but with the performance phrases of the instrumentalists, the questioner, and the storyteller-singer. In addition, in the slot between the end of one choral ostinato and the beginning of the next, a supporting singer many also perform an ostinato that responds to the chorus. Once the performance is moving quite smoothly, another group, the "muu-raising-people," may enter to interlock yet another pattern.

Figure 2. Responding Underneath People and Song Catcher, Episode 2

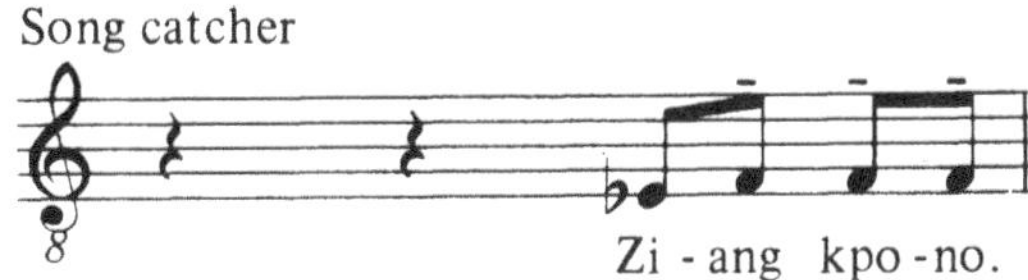

The musical backdrop becomes pervasive and distinctive in the event. Though the music is endlessly repetitive, the audience comprehends it as joined with the narrative stream or song of the storyteller-singer. As the story changes, the music changes and colors the total impression. Never does one think of the teller as just telling the epic, for the music is an essential and core part.

The epic singer finds a questioner (mare-kẹẹ-kẹ-nuu) among the crowd to pose the crucial questions throughout and to create a dialogue with the singer as he moves through his story. The questioner prods the epic singer at crucial points, asking who is speaking or wondering out loud how such a fantastic thing could have, in fact, happened. As questioner he represents the audience, speaking what others are thinking and creating comic scenes with his commentary on what is happening. His part removes the storyteller-singer from being a lone actor and sets up a crucial transactional approach to the performance.

The other members of the audience also serve to make the epic event very much of a dialogic event. They call and respond to each other and to the epic singer in intricately dovetailed patterns. The chorus converses with the epic singer. Yet within the chorus the main group carries on a sub-conversation with the supporting singer. In a similar way, the instrumentalists respond to one another and in turn together fit into the chorus and epic singer conversation. Figure 3 illustrates the basic dialogues that build in epic and that affect and shape the unfolding of time in the event.

The epic singer fashions his performance by "tuning in" his chorus and instrumentalists. To do this he first demonstrates each part and then sings with the appropriate performers as he adds and layers them into their slots. Gradually, the increasing ensemble becomes more adept and smooth in their ever-repeating and interwoven parts. Only then does the epic singer launch into his own singing and narrating role. But if things falter even for a time, he quickly switches back to being conductor and once more guides the ensemble. He even prompts the questioner if he doesn't ask questions at the critical and pivotal points in the narrative.

As the epic singer tells his story, lapsing every few sentences into song to punctuate his rendition, he is kneeling. From this position he gestures, imitates, and points with his upper body. His motions are as appreciated as his words and they add an arresting dimension to his artistry. By lantern and firelight these movements become exaggerated in the shadows, often assuming gigantic and grotesque proportions.

Figure 3. Dialogic Relationships in Kpelle Epic

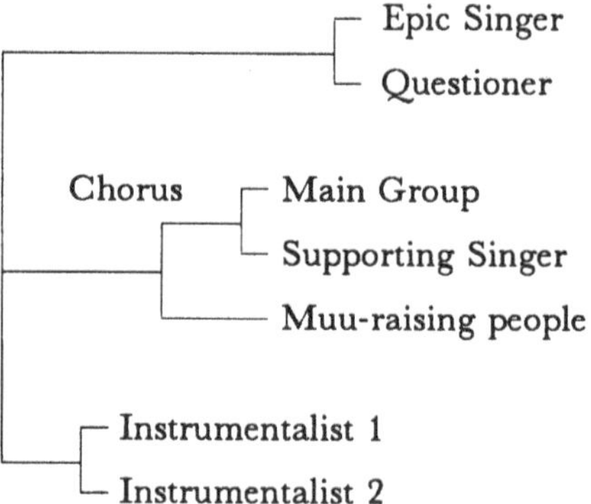

Exaggeration, lies, and absurd situations characterize the epic. The audience delights in all these and openly laughs. Epic is comic and people come to a performance expecting hilarity. While some humor is associated with the characters that are chosen, much results from the timing and skill that the singer shows. He must compose his rendition from a large stock of phrases, words, and songs. Much of what he does in the nuance is the result of momentary and quick decisions, for which he has developed the instinct from long practice.

A PERFORMANCE WITHOUT END

Wọi-mẹni-pele, or epic, resembles in some ways the mẹni-pele (chante fable). Both are narratives grounded by an ever-present chorus. However, the wọi-mẹni-pele features the central Wọi character in each and every episode, while mẹni-pele may depict a variety of characters, not necessarily related to those in the previous mẹni-pele. Also, wọi-mẹni-pele emphasizes an event in which the narrative never concludes. As one performer told his audience as an aside,

"You yourself the head of an epic does not come out. You just keep bouncing." The singer realizes this goal of a never-ending story by constructing each episode so that a neat conclusion is never reached. Rather, in the midst of an episode the elements of a future episode are inserted. Textually, and sometimes musically, this is done as phrases of an upcoming episode are introduced before a current episode has ended. Toward the end of Episode Two, for example, Kulung sings the choral response of the upcoming Episode Three to weld the two more firmly together (see fig. 4).

Figure 4. Foreshadowing in Epic, Episode 2

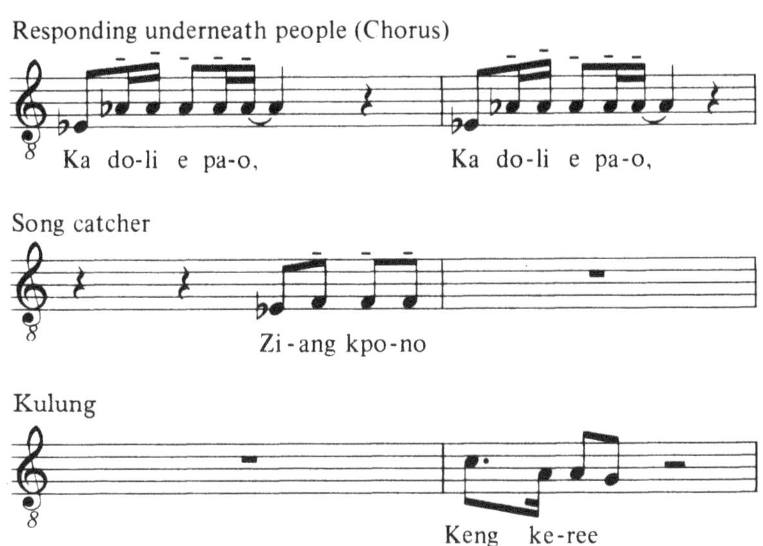

Toward the end of Episode Four (Tuu-tuu-Bird Pumps Bellows), Kulung abruptly begins an entirely new topic:

Nar. He said, "It is a good matter." He said, "Then the way this war is hot," one of his wives is there. He said, "Wife?"
She said, "Ee."
He said, "You."
She said, "Mm."
He said, "You say I don't love you, then go and sit at the fork of the big road. Carve bowls there with your voice. . . ."

Shortly thereafter, the episode ends and it is only with the beginning of the next (Jealous Wife Carves Bowls) that we see the unfolding of this topic.

Right before the end of Episode Seven (House Meets Bẹlẹ) the theme of the next episode (Lizard is Struck) is inserted, as the narrator hints:

> The bow has talked, the arrow has talked. All have songs. I'll come there.

The next episode opens with the iron bow and arrow theme.

Time shifts occur even in the narrative text, for the teller, as often as sentence to sentence, moves to various times, revealing the action of the story. The temporal style in the Kpelle epic contrasts with that of the chante fable, where each story-song concludes rather neatly after a dramatic highpoint. As Kpelle people readily articulate, the epic must not end. Its construction should create the impression that it goes on forever. The careful hinting of future action in a present episode serves to obscure otherwise demarcated episodes. In the example described here, the evening's performance ends as a battle is building up as the beautiful Poling-Bird is stalking Gemila.

The modes of performance—song and narrative—are not completely isolated one from another. The song relates, though frequently allusively, to the narrative theme. Even the syllables of the choral ostinato are chosen to represent a symbolic reference to the narrative. To that end, the dramatic highpoint dovetails with the beginnings of the next small plot, muting the segmentation. On a basic level, the wọi-mẹni-pele is a more extended event. It is performed as a full evening's entertainment with possible continuation on subsequent evenings. The mẹni-pele can be performed as a few self-contained modules that preface another event. The epic episodes presented here, therefore, are in no respect to be considered a complete epic as we might think of it. Rather, they are a sample of the kind of episodes that might occur, and they are extracted from an actual performance in the order in which they were performed.

The Wọi epic, significantly, has no precise starting or concluding episode. Unlike the Mwindo epic recorded by Daniel Biebuyck and Kahombo Mateene among the Nyanga people (1971), the Wọi epic does not proceed from the birth of the hero through his various lifetime adventures. Rather, from all evidence, the teller is free to begin at any point and end at any point. This, according to the Kpelle, underscores the very continuity of the event. For example, Episode Five in this performance, the banishment of the jealous wife to carve bowls, becomes the first episode in another of Kulung's renditions.

SETTING AND CHARACTERS

The epic takes place in the distant past, as implied by the episode in which all living things—plants and animals—are born to Wọi's wife. It is also set in a time of fighting and conflict, as Wọi, the hero, moves from one battle to another. The episodes included here move between earth and various parts of the sky: the part of the sky upon which one can sit (ɣele-kọlọng), and the distant sky which exists behind the sky proper (ɣele-polu).

The central characters are Wọi and his family: his wives, his sister, his daughter (Maa-pu), and his two sons (Zu-kpeei, the elder, and Wọi-boi, the younger). Divinities include two monster spirits who oppose Wọi: Ɣele-lawọ, who appears also as a bitter rattan plant, and Mẹni-maa-fa, who sometimes becomes a lizard and who married Wọi's sister. A number of animals are featured characters in the epic as well: Tuu-tuu-Bird, who pumps the bellows for forging a needle to sew Wọi's war clothes; greedy Spider, who plays the slit drum so that bellows can be pumped; as well as Squirrel-Monkey, Beetle, Bat, Bull, the bees, and others. Plants of importance include Bẹlẹ and Koing trees as well as Pumpkin and Koong leaf, the latter used to thatch houses. In addition, certain objects become actors and assume human qualities. These include Bow and Arrow, Bag, Axe, and Cutlass. Certain characters simultaneously belong to different realms and exhibit a complex of features blurring the distinctions drawn here between animal, plant, and human realms. Mẹni-maa-fa, for example, is both a monster spirit and a lizard. His lizardness indicates how he moves and operates, his spirit nature allows him extraordinary power. Actors also include the tutelary and other spirits who are invoked by the singer to be present at the performance, though they are not central to the epic plot itself.

PLOT

The plot in the performance under analysis unfolds in seventeen episodes. A brief synopsis follows:

Episode 1: Wọi prepares for war. Squirrel-Monkey, Tsetse-Fly, and Horse-Fly join him to go to Ɣele-lawọ, who has taken one of Wọi's bulls.

Episode 2: The diviner of the anteater's hole is called to predict the future as Wọi's wife gives birth to all living things.

Episode 3: A feast is cooked for Spider, one of the things born of Wọi's wife, so that he can play the slit drum and make music for pumping the bellows and forging the needle to make Wọi's battle clothes.

Episode 4: Tuu-tuu-Bird arrives to pump the bellows, and Beetle to forge the iron for the needle. Tuu-tuu-Bird has sleeping sickness, however, and keeps dozing at his work.

Episode 5: Wọi bans one of his wives, who is jealous of co-wives, to the fork of the road outside town. There she carves bowls, using her voice. The male clients she solicits pay her by sleeping with her.

Episode 6: Wọi's house is moving into battle. The various creatures—rooster and frogs—sing praises as it moves.

Episode 7: Wọi's sons, Zu-kpeei and Wọi-boi, attempt to cut down Bẹlẹ-Tree, which is blocking the passage of the moving house. Wọi's daughter waits to set fire to the tree when it falls. As the tree falls, Mẹni-maa-fa, in the form of a lizard, slaps the tree with its head and restores it. Wọi gives his son a bow and arrow to assist him in overcoming the lizard.

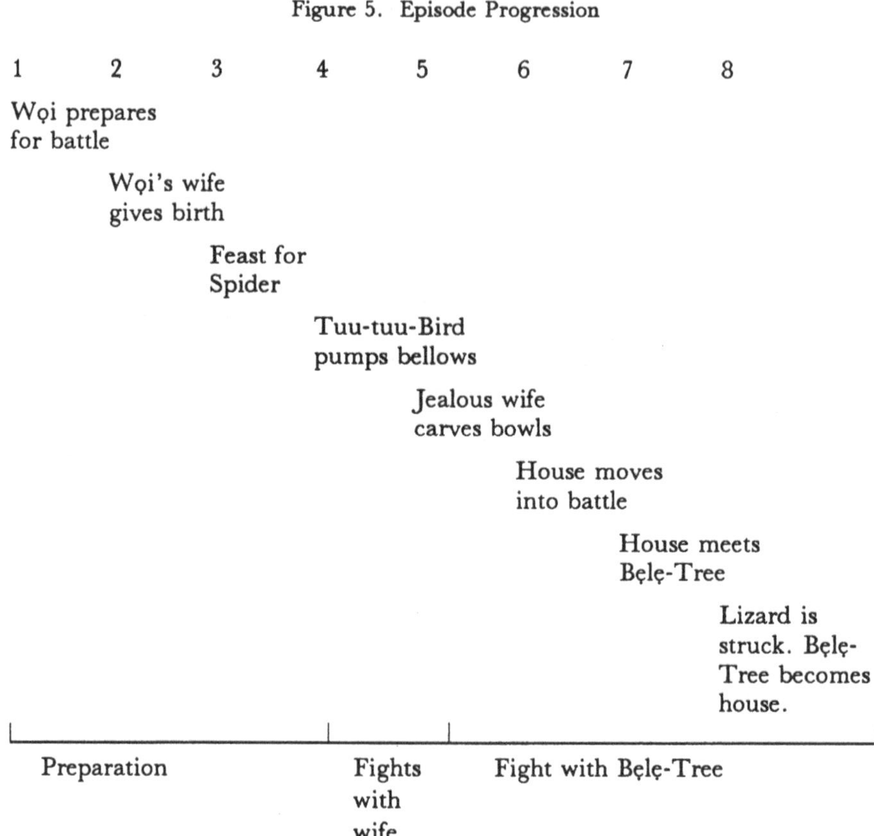

Figure 5. Episode Progression

Episode 8: Lizard emerges and Bow comes to life, sending an arrow to strike the lizard down. Bẹlẹ-Tree flies from where it is standing to become one of Wọi's houses.

Episode 9: The house of the transformed Bẹlẹ travels toward the distant sky, the house containing all people.

Episode 10: The house arrives at the base of Koing-Tree and cannot pass this obstacle. Wọi reaches into his bag and brings forth Axe and Cutlass, who are there to help him.

Episode 11: Cutlass proceeds to chop Koing-Tree, and Axe to split it. The tree is cleared and Mẹni-maa-fa moves to try and remove his wife, Wọi's sister, from the house. Mẹni-maa-fa meets Bat, enlisting his help to retrieve his wife.

Episode 12: Bat prepares to assault the house, but as Wọi holds out Koong-Leaf, Bat enters it and is caught. The house moves forward.

Figure 5. Episode Progression

9	10	11	12	13	14	15	16	17
House moves								
	House arrives at Koing-Tree							
		Cutlass and Axe chop Koing-Tree						
			Bat assaults house and is caught					
				Pumpkin is placed to block house				
					Knife cuts Pumpkin			
						Poling-Bird fights Gemila		
Fights Koing-Tree			Fights Bat	Fights Pumpkin		Poling fights Gemila		

Episode 13: The house is moving and Mẹni-maa-fa rushes ahead to find Pumpkin. Pumpkin agrees to help him by swelling up so that the house cannot pass. Wọi hits his bag once again for help.

Episode 14: Double-edged Knife splits Pumpkin and the house passes.

Episode 15: The beautiful, smart Poling-Bird meets Gemila, who is powerful and plucks out people's eyes.

Episode 16: Gemila goes about plucking out eyes and Wọi becomes angry because people are sitting and allowing it to happen. Poling agrees to fight Gemila and the people dress her up in finery and she steps outside.

Episode 17: Poling is outside stalking and waiting to confront Gemila.

THE THEME OF CONFLICT

The episodes involve conflicts of various types. The most prominent conflict is between Wọi and his enemies as he tries to move his house toward the sky. Family conflict develops from the actions of Mẹni-maa-fa, an adversary who puts numerous roadblocks in Wọi's path. Mẹni-maa-fa is a monster spirit who married Wọi's sister by disguising himself as a human. When he reveals his true nature, his wife leaves him and returns to Wọi, the cause of Mẹni-maa-fa's anger against Wọi. Family conflict erupts also in the form of jealousy by a wife whom Wọi bans to the edge of town. It is important to note, however, that as the epic is performed, the actual conflict and fighting are not emphasized. The drama of battle is quite absent. Dramatic moments when the enemy is defeated appear muted. In such a way, climax and time moving toward a climax are not fundamentally important. Indeed, sometimes threads of a conflict appear that are never resolved. In the first episode, for example, Wọi is preparing to fight Ɣele-lawọ and yet, after preparations are made, he goes off to fight Mẹni-maa-fa instead. As Kpelle people point out, such a performance does not indicate incompetence on the narrator's part. Rather, it shows that action can be started for which a conclusion may or may not be reached. The epic ideally reveals many small plots, the resolution of which is not essential within a single performance. In fact, to have many themes going is to create the rich texture so desirable. The audience delights in the small twists the narrator employs to connect different themes. For example, in the third episode, the common motif of Spider's greed, which is ubiquitous in Kpelle folklore, becomes integrated into the story of Wọi as Spider plays the music necessary to make war preparations. Later, in the eighth episode, after the lizard is overpowered, the Bẹlẹ-Tree blocking the house's path is transformed into the house itself. Thus the tree becomes interconnected with the hero Wọi.

The plot of the epic as performed here does not move to a single climactic battle. Rather, it continues with a series of battles, one not more important than another. Four episodes are devoted to war preparation, one to a jealous wife, three to fighting the Bẹlẹ-Tree, three to conquering the Koing-Tree, one to overcoming the bat, and two to beating the pumpkin. All of this serves to reinforce the notion of circularity, for one does not identify a single important moment, a climax, toward which all actions build.

The lack of plot movement, however, does not mean lack of action. Movement and action are depicted with precise characterization throughout the episodes. The actions depicted include playing the slit drum, pumping the bellows, carving bowls, cutting trees. Movement and walking are even more ubiquitously portrayed in Episodes Six and Nine, which are devoted almost exclusively to depicting the movement of the house as it goes forward and comes back, shakes, and proceeds ahead. Such stress on portrayal of action is congruous with a general emphasis on quality of movement in Kpelle life.

VARIATIONS IN THE WỌI EPIC

The question might be raised as to the extent of variations within this epic from one narrator to another. Research and interviews have revealed some interesting similarities and variants. The house that moves is quite common to the versions in the central Kpelle area. The conflict within the family is also typical. In some versions the creation episode is told not about Wọi's wife but about Wọi's mother giving birth to all things. In the latter version, Wọi is the lastborn and thus endowed with all the cumulative power of those born before. If the lastborn child is a girl, the Kpelle say, "That's our mother." If it is a boy, they say, "That's our father."

The iron-forging episode is common, and invariably the bellows pumper is not able to do a very efficient job. Instead of the sleeping bird, other versions include a frog with short hands that cause difficulty in pumping. In some versions sparks from the fire fall on the frog's back causing the spots visible on many frogs today.

Obstacles that Wọi meets may be any of many kinds of trees. There may also be obstacles of other kinds. In one version, Wọi's house meets an anthill. To pass the anthill, Wọi enlists the aid of an anteater and a mole who work in tandem to dig the earth and make a tunnel beneath the ground where the house can pass.

While some versions incorporate different characters or objects, others simply elaborate details of common objects in a way missing from other versions. For example, one performer elaborated that Wọi's bow required two hundred people to pick it up. The arrow required one hundred and fifty people. Yet another narrator said that Mẹni-maa-fa's backbone was so tall that it reached to the sky, blocking Wọi's path. Axe and Cutlass were enlisted to chop the backbone.

CHAPTER 2

The Wọi Epic

Against a rich background of music—vocal and instrumental—the text of the Wọi epic builds. To give a flavor of that text, I present the translation of seventeen episodes performed by Kulung on one particular occasion. This constitutes a representative sample, not the complete epic, for the Kpelle do not think in finite terms about the Wọi epic. What the Kpelle hear in a single performance, or what is given here, is but a fraction of the larger, never-concluding corpus.

The story presented here was recorded on audiotape one market day in Totota, Liberia, where an eager crowd from surrounding villages joined the event. On other occasions we also videotaped Kulung performing the epic. I consider this typical of the performances he created and the reactions he engendered in audiences.

The text is visually organized to illustrate a number of temporal flows that the storyteller-singer establishes and among which he moves, sometimes with surprising rapidity and frequency. Text set in the position to the far left helps establish and reassert the frame of epic as a style of performance. Certain characteristic phrases are markers or cues to phases within that epic. As the episode begins, the mare-kẹẹ-kẹ-nuu asks, "Whose song is that?" With that prompting but not before, the storyteller launches the narrative. At the end of an episode, the storyteller-singer says, "Dried millet, wẹsẹ [sound of breaking]," and the chorus responds, "Wẹsẹ [sound of breaking]," for the formulaic termination. The singer also gives explanations about why certain things are done in the epic. At times he levels criticism at the performers. All this serves to define epic as a kind of performance.

Text set in the middle position is the narrative stream within the epic. Here is found the bulk of interaction between characters. While the storyteller-singer produces most of this, the questioner also enters into the narrative stream with his questions and comments.

Text in the extreme right-hand position is sung by the "pourer" (storyteller-singer). Here we find the most esoteric and abstract ideas. Proverbial phrases and formulas, some that are found in other Kpelle music, lace this text. The words to the signature tune of each episode are also placed in this position. The chorus continues the signature tune after the pourer demonstrates it. Only Kulung, however, inserts the heart and soul of the epic, the proverbs and other nuggets of "deep" Kpelle.

Striking in the text are the many "backstage" elements and construction details of the performance. More than with a single song, the superstructure of the larger event becomes part of the expression production.

EPISODE 1

Wọi Prepares for Battle

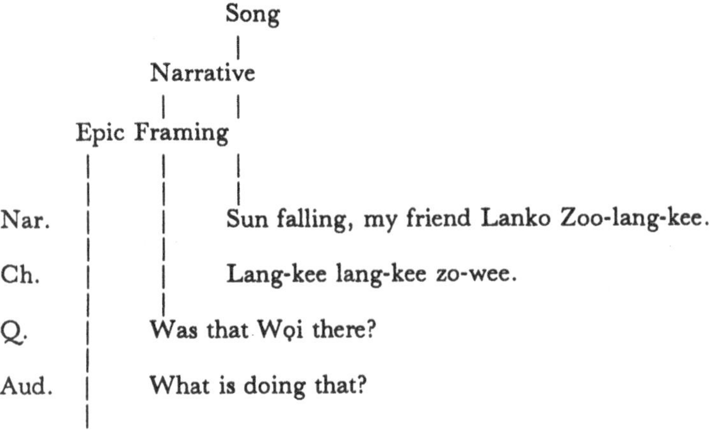

Nar. Let the song agree, let the song agree, gently.

Wọi said, "That's fine." He said, "That's fine, then I'm ready for the fight." They said to him, "Then the song is put down, and you want to start the fight in the song?" He said, "Then what will I do?"

Young man answer, you all answer well. Answer well. Answer well, and I'll sing the song well, and we'll see what they will do.

Ee, Maa-laa doesn't fool around, Zoo-lang-kee.[2]
Oh, they have treated me badly, Zoo-lang-kee.
Sun-falling-foolish-dancer doesn't know a bad place, Zoo-lang-kee.
Va, va, va, va, va, va, va, va, va, va, va, va, va, va, va, va, va, va, va, va, va, va. [sound of walking]

Wọi is ready. He said, "You singing that, Zoo-lang-kee, the war is ready."

2. Names Maa-laa and Zoo-lang-kee are often references to a tutelary spirit or deceased performer invoked throughout the event to provide force and clarity for the storyteller.

And I was in the house. I said to him, "Ee." I said to him, "Wọi?"[3]
He said to me, "Mm."
I said to him, "What war is prepared? You yourself see the sitting-on-the-neck crowd here. Why is the war being prepared since there is no one equal to you?" "Fine, when Kelema-ninga has pumped my bellows and they have forged my needle and they have sewn my clothes, then we will start on the war."
My in-law isn't that right?
Ee, Maa-laa doesn't fool around, Zoo-lang-kee.
Sun-falling, they have treated me badly, Zoo-lang-kee.
Oh, I'm the one who gave your feast, Zoo-lang-kee.
Wọi, I'm the one who worked for you, Zoo-lang-kee.
Ee, Wọi is dancing, oh Zoo-lang-kee.
Squirrel-Monkey has come out kili, kili, kili, kili.
Squirrel monkey, explain it to the woman. A small monkey that they call lele. Explain it to the woman.

Aud. She understands it.

Nar. They came to Squirrel-Monkey. Squirrel-Monkey said, "Fine. I'm coming to Wọi's place so that we, so that I can fight."
They said to him, "What do you do in the fight?"
"I take a person up a dry tree."
One man called Ɣele-lawọ has caught one of Wọi's bulls and raised it behind the sky. And when you are going to Ɣele-lawọ's place, Squirrel-Monkey must climb in the dry tree quietly and get down behind the sky.

Q. Were you near there?

Nar. Very close.
Oh, Maa-laa bring my voice, oh my people.
Oh, they have treated me badly, Zoo-lang-kee.
Sun-falling, I'm the one who worked for you, Zoo-lang-kee.
Oh, I'm the one who worked for you, Zoo-lang-kee.
Ee-oh, I'm the one who did your performance, Zoo-lang-kee.
Wọi-wee, I'm the one who did your work, Zoo-lang-kee.
Sun-falling, they have treated me badly, Zoo-lang-kee.
Maa-laa doesn't fool around, Zoo-lang-kee.
Squirrel-Monkey was coming, Squirrel-Monkey was coming

3. Here Wọi speaks to the narrator and brings him into the scene of the epic. Such a device provides veracity for the teller's assertion that he, in fact, witnessed those things of which he tells.

very fast. He said, "Then, Wọi, the battle is in your wings."
Tsetse-Fly has come.
He said to him, "I'm with you."

Name all the things for the woman.

Behold, Horse-Fly has come. He said to him, "I'm in your wings." Horse-Fly has come. He said to him, "I'm in your wings so that we may fight the war, because Ɣele-lawọ, the way he is boastful. . . . And at Ɣele-lawọ's place, a big bull is there. And cows, bees drop on the horns.

Explain it to the woman.

Bees have entered the horns and they are very honeyed, I tell you. The honey was dripping.

Aud. Just keep telling, the explaining time is there. When you have finished.

Nar. Ee, Maa-laa-ke-ma doesn't fool around.
Sun-falling, ee Maa-laa bring my voice.
Sun-falling, ee Maa-laa bring my voice.
Sun-falling solo catcher.
Va, va, va, fast, fast, fast, fast, fast, fast.

Q. What is doing that ee?

Nar. Va, va, va, va, va, va, va, va, va, va, va, fast, va, va, va, va, va, va, va, va.

Ɣele-lawọ is ready. He is ready to take him behind the sky immediately so that they can put the big bull down before the battle begins.

Va, va, va, va, va, va, va, va, va, va, va, va.

Squirrel-Monkey has come. He said, "Wọi?"
He said to him, "Ee."
He said to him, "All right, climb behind the sky."
He said to him, "How can I climb there?"
He said to him, "I climb there with your voice."
Wọi climbed, Wọi climbed, Wọi climbed, Wọi climbed, Wọi climbed. Wọi has arrived behind the sky, the bull has gotten down.
The bull is really tall, the bees were on its horns.

Ee, Maa-laa doesn't fool around.
Sun-falling, they have treated me badly.
Foolish-dancer doesn't know a bad place.[4]
Sun Maa-laa, wee.

---

4. A proverb referring to the fact that a bad performer is so bad that he or she doesn't pay attention to audience response and dances indiscriminately anywhere.

Oh, they are fooling us, Zoo-lang-kee.
Dried millet, wẹsẹ.

Aud. Wẹsẹ.

EPISODE 2

Wọi's Wife Gives Birth

Nar. Go call the diviner to come.[5]
Ziang-kpono.
Call him to come.
Go call the diviner to come.

Ch. Ziang-kpono.

Nar. Call him to come.

S.S. [Supporting Singer]
Call him to come.

Ch. Ziang-kpono.

Nar. Answer that song well.
Ee, what does the diviner say?
Go, call the diviner from the anteater's hole to come.
Ee, Maa-laa bring my voice.
Go, call the diviner to come.
Sun-falling, oh.
Go, call the diviner to come.
Stop, you hitting it, hold it in your hand. Pass it on the direction of the mouth [opening].
Iron doesn't like Left-behind.[6]
Cut it short, short, let's go.
Hold it like rice and its tying rope.[7]
Go, call the diviner to come.
Oh, diviner, what do you say?
My people, don't respond with your bad voice. Don't make my heart hurt in my stomach, man.

Aud. I want to do two things. I want to really understand it.

---

5. Divination is used by Kpelle people as an important means of taking action in relation to the future. Thus, with the pregnancy of Wọi's wife, advice is sought.

6. A proverb referring to people clearing bush in a work cooperative where everyone is to keep pace with his fellow worker as the group cuts a swath through the forest. Here the proverb is used to chide members of the chorus who are lagging behind the rest of the group.

7. Another proverbial expression referring to the fact that the rice stalk must be held in one hand while the other hand holds the tying string in a specific manner. The singer is again referring to the chorus and their need to do things in the proper way.

Nar. My fellow, answer man, answer man.

It's the diviner of the hole that they are calling.

It was Wọi's wife who was pregnant, and they are calling diviner from the anteater's hole.

You, yourself, the head of an epic doesn't come out. You just keep bouncing.

They are going for divination. And the diviner of the anteater's hole is in the road. He comes to him and says to him, "Then here I am."

"Come and divine for me."

Ee, what does Maa-laa-ke-ma say?

Go, call the diviner of the anteater's hole to come.

Go, call the diviner of the anteater's hole to come.

Boys answer, boys answer, boys answer. Take your hand out of your mouth.

Oh, what does Maa-laa say?

Wọi's wife was pregnant kpung-kung. And that is why they were going for divination.

Q. What did you say?

Nar. They have gone to the diviner of the anteater's hole.

He said, "Then, that's fine. Oh, is the pregnant woman coming for divination? Then it is a matter that . . . so, ah woman." He said, "Then woman . . . she will give birth right now. Just cut a road."

At that time there was nothing alive.[8]

Sheep didn't exist. Chickens didn't exist. There was nothing at all alive.

Q. Are you telling the truth?

Nar. Very close. Her stomach reached to the ocean.

Q. Were you near?

Nar. Very close.

Ah-oh, what does the diviner say?

Go, call the diviner of the anteater's hole to come.

I tell you the stomach. They said, "Cut a road."[9]

---

8. In this episode a cursory account is given of how life was created. One of Wọi's wives was responsible for the feat.

9. This refers to the path cut from the village to the shelter where a woman may be secluded during labor.

The woman was delivering I tell you. People are coming, chickens, ducks, sheep, goats, all, all are coming. The only things left are Spider and Slit-Drum. Slit-Drum has come.[10]

Q. My friend, what are you telling me?

Nar. Keng-keree, eh.[11]
Dried millet, wẹsẹ.

Ch. Wẹsẹ.

EPISODE 3

Feast for Spider

Nar. Keng-keree, ee.[12]

Aud. Ask the questions.

Nar. Ee keng-keree doo wee taya.
Ee keng-keree,

Ch. Doo wee taya.

Nar. Ee keng-keree,

Ch. Doo wee taya.

Nar. Ee keng-keree,

Ch. Doo wee taya.

Nar. Answer the song well so that my bad name doesn't remain with the woman.
Because the thing, the thing I did of old.

Aud. Ask the question.

Q. Whose voice is that?

Aud. Bring that thing, let me play it.

Q. Don't lie to me here.

---

10. This foreshadows the next episode, where Spider becomes the central figure.

11. This musical phrase is the core of the next episode and becomes dovetailed before the closing formula.

12. Imitation of the sound of playing the slit drum. "Keng kere" also means the sound of something large. "Doo wee taya" imitates the sound of something scattering, all referring to the enormous quantity of food being placed all around.

Nar. Very close. Lying, I lie to you? Isn't it piassava that has split over me?[13] I, Kulung, have they ever called me there?

Q. What thing's song is that again?

Nar. Spider, Father-Spider. He's the one playing the Slit-Drum.
He's playing the Slit-Drum, and they surround him with food.
He eats, he plays the Slit-Drum.[14]

Q. Will you do its imitation so that we can see?

Nar. I will do the imitation for you to see right now.

They cooked rice, they set it out. They cooked sweet potatoes, they set them out. They cut cassava, they set it out. They cooked eddoes, they set them out. Every kind of food they circled round him. As he eats, he plays the Slit-Drum.

Q. Will he eat all the things himself?

Nar. Completely, by himself.

Keapee, I see you, Keapee, I see you.
Blackbird, did you sleep well?

Respond well to the song.

Q. Let me sit within your gaze to see.

Nar. Let me turn toward your eyes myself.

Q. Don't lie to me.

Nar. Kereng, ting, ting. Ting-king kiling, kiling, kiling, kiling, kiling, kiling.
Ting-king kiling, kiling, kiling, kiling, kiling, kiling.
Ting-king kiling, kiling, kiling, kiling. Ting-king.
Ting-king kiling. Kiling, kiling, kiling. Kiling, kiling, kiling.
Ting-king, king. Kiling ting, king, king, king.
Kiling, ting, king, king, king.

Q. What is he doing?

Nar. He's eating the things and playing the Slit-Drum.

---

13. To say that "piassava has split over me" implies that a very important thing has happened, which may either be good or bad.

14. The character of the greedy spider is ubiquitous not only in Kpelle but in many West African narratives, as is the trickster. Spider is also attributed by the Kpelle to be a musician. In addition to the slit drum, the Kpelle say that when one lies in bed one can sometimes hear what sounds like a spider beating the hourglass drum, though he makes the sound as he walks. To hear such music is a bad sign and a sign that something disastrous is about to happen.

Bird-wee, keng-keree.
Oh Bird-wee, keng-keree.
Sun-falling Maa-Laa, keng-keree.
Blackbird, did you sleep well, oh, keng-keree.
Maa-zoo, did you sleep well, oh, keng-keree.

Keapee look at me, Keapee look at me, Keapee look at me, Keapee look at me, Keapee look at me, Keapee look at me, Keapee look at me. I didn't know this place. Wake up.

Bang, bang, bang, bang, bang, bang, bang, bang, bang.[15]

Q. My friend, what does that? What thing are you doing?

Nar. Ee Bird-wee, keng-keree.
Ee Bird-wee, keng-keree.
Maa-zoo, did you sleep well, oh, keng-keree.

Q. But they will not forge this iron today.

Nar. Oo-ee-oo, keng-keree.
Ee, Maa-laa-ke-ma, oh, keng-keree.
Blackbird, did you sleep well, oh keng-keree. Kereng, ting, ting, ting, ting, ting, ting, ting, ting, ting.
Ting-king, kiling, kiling, kiling, kiling, kiling, kiling, kiling, kiling, kiling, kiling, kiling, kiling.
Tini-kiling, ting-king, kiling, kiling, kiling, kiling.
Ting-kiling, ting-king, kiling.
Tini-king, kiling. Ting-kiling, ting, ting, kiling, ting-king.

Q. Are those the things he is eating?

Nar. Those are the things he is eating.
Kereng, ting, ting.

Q. Kulung, don't lie to me here.

Nar. I'm not lying.

Q. They say you really lie.

Nar. He said, "The people caught me here to play the slit drum.
Wọi brought me here and the food isn't adequate."
They said, "Cook new rice."

Q. Is he hungry?

Nar. He is hungry.

15. The imitation of forging iron foreshadows the episode that follows.

Q. Has he finished that enormous amount of food?

Nar. Ee Bird-wee, keng-keree.
Ee Bird-wee, keng-keree.
Oh, keng-keree.
Maa-zoo, did you sleep well, keng-keree.
Oh, Bird-wee keng-keree.
Blackbird, come and see me, see me, see me.
The Poro is on a person, the matter angers him.[16]
Night falls on him, the daylight bewitches him.
The large, large rooster, the hen's voice is sweet, the rooster crows the dawn.[17]
We are going to Totota, oh yes.
I'm going to Totota, oh yes.
I'm going to Totota, oh yes.
Ee, Maa-laa-ke-ma, oh, my people, oh.

Q. But Spider is not going to play Wọi's Slit-Drum today.

Nar. Ah, the food they are making! They are cooking rice again and packing it. And Wọi is lying in the sky.

Aud. What is he going to do?

Nar. When Spider is full, then Wọi will get out of the sky and get down. Then the war is ready.

Q. Don't lie to me.

Nar. Very close. I can't do that.
Wọi has now done it, Spider's rice. They set out the rice, eddoes, sweet potatoes, ripe bananas. All things they circle around him.

Aud. What is he going to do with it?

Nar. He will eat it and play the Slit-Drum. When he is full, then the war has started up. And Wọi's bellows of which they long

---

16. A proverb of numerous possible meanings. Related to the epic it applies to Spider, who sits there without enough food to satisfy him. He is, however, obliged to play and is not able to show his anger. This is similar to the Poro's disciplining a person, a matter which cannot be questioned. Spider's situation is also compared to morning coming before a person has realized the night is there. Spider, in other words, cannot deal with one hardship before another arrives.

17. This proverb shows yet another way of expressing the dilemma in which Spider finds himself. Even though a hen has the finer voice, it is the rooster who gets the honor of announcing the morning. Thus the person most deserving may not always be the one rewarded, and this emphasizes the paradox of Spider's situation. Though he plays well, his reward is determined by the generosity of the people serving him.

ago spoke. The clothes that are on him. Kelema-ninga is there. He is the one who will forge the needle in order for them to pump the bellows.

Ee, Bird-wee, keng-keree.
Blackbird, how did you sleep, keng-keree?
Sun-falling Maa-laa-ke-ma, oh, keng-keree.
A dancer doesn't stand outside.
Then she has broken the law.[18]

Initiated ones, thank you, thank you, thank you, thank you. That's the song, that's the song, that's the song, that's the song, that's the song.

Ki-ting, ting, ting, ting, ting, ting, ting, ting, king,
kiling, ting-kiling, ting-king kiling, ting-king kiling,
kiling, kiling, kiling, kiling, kiling, kiling, kiling, kiling,
kiling, kiling, kiling, kiling, kiling, kiling, kiling, kiling.

Aud. What is doing that?

Nar. The Slit-Drum he's playing, Wọi was in the sky dancing.

Q. Oh, my friend.

Nar. King kiling, kiling, king kiling, king kiling, ting-king,
ting-king kiling, kereng, kiling-ting, kiling-ting, tenge,
tenge, kiling, kereng, kiling, ting-king.

Aud. Will he play the Slit-Drum today?

Nar. Ting-king, ting-king.
Blackbird, how did you sleep?

Q. Isn't Spider full yet?

Nar. He's not yet full. You yourself, those things would do what to Spider?
He said, "That's fine."
Then Spider can't blame me.
He said, "That's fine. Then what can I tell him about my needle forging matter?"

Keapee, do you see me?
Do you see me, oh, keng-keree?
Keapee, do you see me, keng-keree?
Keapee, do you see me, keng-keree?
Ee Maa-laa, keng-keree.
Sun-falling itself there, oh, keng-keree.

---

18. Another reference to Spider's lack of recourse in his anger. He, as a skilled musician, is obliged like a dancer to perform when the occasion arises, despite anger or dissatisfaction.

There is a large gown. It came from Ɣele-lawọ, it came down "pau." Wọi said, "Then sew my clothes. As soon as I've put them on, we will fight."

Q. Wọi and who will fight the war?

Nar. He and Ɣele-lawọ.

Ee, Bird-wee, people.

All right, the person sewing the clothes. Wọi said to him, "Then that's fine." He said to him, "Are these the clothes you are going to sew?"

He said, "Yes."

He said to him, "Then these clothes, these clothes you want to sew, if you sew them, I wear them, then you won't have to fight. But all you people here, we are all going to fight at Ɣele-lawọ's place because Ɣele-lawọ is fierce, he doesn't fool around. All right, Kpayang-miling, that's the name of Beetle.

Q. They call it what?

Nar. Kpayang-miling.

Q. Is that the name of Beetle?

Nar. That's the name of Beetle. Kelema-ninga, that is him there. That is Tuu-tuu-Bird. And he is the one who has sleeping sickness badly. He is pumping the bellows so they can forge the needle and sew the clothes.

Dried millet, wẹsẹ.

Ch. Wẹsẹ.

EPISODE 4

Tuu-tuu-Bird Pumps Bellows

Nar. Kelema-ninga blow it, zang kali ma zang, blow it.
Kelema-ninga, blow it.

Ch. Zang kali ma zang, blow it.

Nar. This song, we didn't raise it up, right?[19]
Those Yilataa people know the song.
Those Yilataa people know the song.
Those Yilataa people know the song.
Ee, Kelema-ninga, gboo.
Blow it, Kelema-ninga, blow it.

---

19. This comment refers to the pitch and timbre of the song. The storyteller wants it at a higher pitch level with a corresponding alteration of timbre.

Oh, Bird-wee, Kelema-ninga, blow it.

Q. Is that Tuu-tuu's name, Kelema-ninga?

Nar. That's Tuu-tuu's name.

Q. And he has come to blow the bellows.

Nar. He has come to blow the bellows and he has sleeping sickness.

Q. And who will forge the iron?

Nar. Kpokiling [a kind of insect].

Q. Oh-h.

Nar. And so they call him Kpayang-miling.

Keapee, look at me, Keapee look at me.
It's just me, it's just me, it's just me.
I, Wawu, it's just me.
Blow it, Kelema-ninga.
Blow it, blow it, Kelema-ninga, blow it.
Oh, ee, oh Kelema-ninga blow it.
Kelema-ninga blow it.
A foolish dancer does not know a bad place.
Ee, Maa-laa-ke-ma, bring my voice.
Oh, Maa-laa-ke-ma, bring my voice.
Ee, oh, Kelema-ninga, blow it.
Blow it, blow it, Kelema-ninga, blow it.
Blow it, blow it, Kelema-ninga, blow it.
This is for me, this is for me, this is for me, this is for me.
Zala keleng, zang, zang keleng, keleng, keleng, keleng, keleng, keleng, keleng, keleng, keleng, keleng, keleng, keleng, keleng.[20]

Q. What is doing that?

Nar. Kelema-ninga is the one that has the sleeping sickness.

Q. And he is the one to blow the bellows.

Nar. Yes, he is afraid of fighting.

Ay-oh, Kelema-ninga-oo.
Ay-oh, Kelema-ninga-oo.
Keleng, zala keleng, zang, zang, keleng, keleng, keleng, keleng, keleng, keleng, zang, zang, keleng, keleng,

20. This imitates the sound of pumping the bellows.

keleng, keleng, keleng, zang, zang, keleng, keleng,
keleng, keleng.

Q. I say, is that the sound of the bellows?

Nar. He has been sitting up and sleeping again. Blow the bellows, blow the bellows. They have awakened him, they have awakened him.

Q. Kelema-Bird, Kelema-Bird.

Nar. They have beaten him on the back and they said to him, "Kelema-Bird, get up."

Q. Kelema-ninga?

Nar. Ee-ee-ee?

Q. Kelema-ninga, what happened?

Nar.
Oh, Keapee, I have come here, oh.
Oh, Keapee, I have come here.
Oh, Keapee, I have come here.
I've come, Keapee, I've come here.
Don't make my voice bad, don't make my voice bad,
don't make my voice bad, don't make my voice bad,
don't make my voice bad.
Respond well, well, well, well, well.
Answer the song well, well, well, well.
Respond well, well, well.
Ee-oh-lee, Kelema-ninga, blow it.
Oh, Bird-wee, Kelema-ninga, blow it.
Zele keleng, kpeng, kpeng, keleng, keleng, veng, veng,
keleng, keleng, zele keleng, zang, zang, keleng, keleng.

Aud. Don't lie to me!

Nar.
Keleng, keleng, keleng, zang, zang, keleng, keleng,
keleng.

Aud. Kelema-ninga! Kelema-ninga!

Nar. Ee-ee-ee.

Q. Will you make the iron red today?

Nar. Oh-h.

Q. But the needle forging time is passing, oh.

Nar.
Oh, Kelema-ninga, oh.
Ay-oh, Kelema-ninga, blow it.
Blow it, blow it, Kelema-ninga, blow it.

Blow it, blow it, Kelema-ninga, blow it.
Blow it, Kelema-ninga, wake up.
Ee, Bird-wee, Kelema-ninga, blow it.
Sun-falling, Kelema-ninga, blow it.
Ee-kee, what does my fellow say, Kelema-ninga blow it.
Kpeng, teng, kpeng, kpeng, kpeng, kpeng, kpeng,
kpeng, kpeng.

Q. Put that one down.[21]

Nar. Ah, we should put it down for nothing? Have I taken the head out yet? You yourself, epic.

Aud. They are hitting it one, one. Hit it quickly.

Nar. You, don't deceive me and my bad name falls, my friend Keapee. The song that I'm singing, am I singing it badly? It is Yilataa where I perform this epic. All of them know it. Ah-ah. Take up that song. But I will take up another one.

Aud. Throw a new one in it.

Q. Throw a new one in it.

Nar. Or doing that, but I'm not yet finished. You told me this.

Q. Kelema-ninga.

Nar. I'm not yet finished with Kelema-ninga.

Aud. Just throw it inside.

Q. Put it inside.

Nar.

Zang gali maa zang, zang gali maa zang.
Oh-koo, Kelema-ninga, blow it.
Oh, Kelema-ninga, blow it.
Ee-oo, Kelema-ninga, blow it.
Oh, Kelema-ninga, blow it.
Blow it, blow it, Kelema-ninga, blow it.
Blow it, blow it, Kelema-ninga, blow it.
Blow it, blow it, Kelema-ninga, blow it.
Ee, Bird-wee, Kelema-ninga, blow it.
Oh, Kelema-ninga, blow it.
Ee-oo, Kelema-ninga, oh.
I am going, oh, Kelema-ninga, oh.

---

21. The questioner wants the singer to stop the present episode and begin a new one. The audience agrees that this one is not going as well as they would like though the narrator protests that he has not yet reached the point he wishes to reach before leaving the episode.

Zele keteng, veng, veng, keleng, keleng, keng, veng, veng, keleng, veng, veng, keleng.

Aud. Will the iron get red hot today?

Nar. Veng, veng, keleng, veng, veng, keleng, zele keteng, zele keteng.

Q. Kelema-ninga! Kelema-ninga!

Nar. Ee-ee-ee.

Q. Are you sleeping?

Nar. Wọi said, "It is a good matter."
Then Kelema-ninga he said, "Mm."
He said, "You."
He said, "Mm."
He said, "You."
He said, "Mm."
He said, "It's you who is not forging the iron so I am not able to go and fight." He said, "You blowing the bellows."
He said, "Mm."
He said, "Then you have sleeping sickness. Let me take the cutlass iron." He took the cutlass iron and rubbed it on his buttocks and he flew.
Tuu-tuu-tuu, that is it, tuu-tuu.[22]

Q. Were you there?

Nar. Very near.

Q. Don't lie to me.

Nar. He said, "It is a good matter." He said, "Then the way this war is hot," one of his wives is there.
He said, "Wife?"
She said, "Ee."
He said, "You."
She said, "Mm."
He said, "You say I don't love you, then go and sit at the fork of the big road.[23] Carve bowls there with your voice in order to make your share of the money inside it, because there are many people surrounding me."

---

22. The voice of Tuu-tuu-Bird.

23. The fork of the road carries a number of meanings. While it is desirable because many people frequent the spot in coming into or going out of town, it is also a location of marginality between forest and town.

Q. She carve what?

Nar. Bowls.

Q. Bowls?

Nar. The bowls they carved long ago.

Q. Wooden bowls?

Nar. Wooden bowls.

Q. That woman is going to carve them?

Nar. The woman will carve the bowl, she will carve it with only her voice.

Q. Oh.

Nar. My in-law, isn't it so?

Aud. We have not yet seen it as truth.

Nar. Dried millet, wẹsẹ.

EPISODE 5

Jealous Wife Carves Bowls

Nar. Respond well, I'll sing the song. I will imitate the things, until whatever happens. All right, that song was with our big voice. Let me raise it in my small voice.

Ee-oo, bowl, mother, mother.

S.S. Ee-oo, bowl, mother, mother.

Ch. Bowl, mother.

Nar. Only the bowl owner knows its price.
I say, it is only the owner who knows its price.
Oh, Maa-laa-ke-ma, we are going, ee.

Q. From whose mouth is that song again?

Nar. One of Wọi's wives is there who is extremely jealous.
He said, "Then let me take you from me. Go and sit at the fork of the road and carve bowls there. Everyone will be buying them."

Q. They will be buying the bowls with what?

Nar. They will buy them on the bed. That woman, you yourself know her ways.

Oh, those who feed him say what?
White bird knows its sitting tree.

Bongkai, kpolong, kpolong, kpolong, kpolong, kpolong,
kpolong, kpolong, kpolong, kpolong, kpolong. Kalu
koro, koro, mọnọ, mọnọ, fẹẹ laa.
Koro, koro, mọnọ, mọnọ, fẹẹ laa.
Koro, koro.[24]

Whose voice is that?

Nar. Flat bowl, bow[24]ed inside.
Shiny black, shiny black bowl. Big bowl.

Q. What does that?

Nar. That's a bowl, oh.
My friend, that is your bowl, oh.
Pass, let's go onto the bed.

Q. Is that the pay?

Nar. I say to you, Wọi's one wife, her lust for men was great. She said to Wọi, "You are not satisfying me."
He said, "Then go sit at the fork of the big road."
She sat at the fork of the road. You, yourself, Wọi is a ritual specialist.

Q. Yes.

Nar. He said to her, "Just carve bowls with your voice."
She carved the bowls with her voice. But she carved the bowls for young men. They just go to the bed.

Q. Then is that the price?

Nar. Then that is the price.
Ee, Maa-laa, what did I say?
Ee-oo, Maa-laa, what did I say?
Only the bowl owner knows its price.
Only the bowl owner knows its price.
Sun-falling, Maa-laa, what do you say?
Bongkai, kpolong, kpolong, kpolong, kpolong, kpolong,
kpolong, kpolong, kpolong, kpolong, kpolong, kpolong,
kpolong, kpolong, kpolong, fẹẹ-laa.
Koro, koro, mọnọ, mọnọ, fẹẹ laa.
Koro, koro, mọnọ, mọnọ, fẹẹ laa.
Bowl flat, bowl well-finished inside, well-finished inside.

---

24. These onomatopoeic terms refer at one level to the various qualities of the bowl being carved, the texture, color, and shape. At a more abstract level they refer to the vagina and the dilemma this jealous woman finds of creating female objects of pleasure for men, the very symbols of her jealousy of other women.

My friend, that is your bowl.
Ee, my friend, pass, let's go to the bed.

Q. What!

Nar. A viking, a viking, a viking, a viking, a viking.

Q. What is happening?

Nar. A viking, a viking.[25]
They have gone to bed.

Q. Oh-koo.

Nar. That's the price for the bowl. That's the song.

Q. Kulung, don't lie to me in this place.

Nar. Very close. Is that an untrue song I am singing? If some of that song is untrue, then some mistake has jumped into it.

I, Tomo-catcher, keep your hand on the song.
Sun-falling Maa-laa doesn't play, oh.
Only the bowl owner knows its price.

They greet that woman. They really greet her. The young men have really come.

Q. What is the name of the woman?

Nar. Ah, Wọi's wife, she has no name. Gelengoi, it's Gelengoi. And if Keapee would greet her, she wouldn't carve her bowl well. Greet the woman then.

Q. I will greet her. "Hello."

Nar. "Who is that? Wait, who is that?"

Q. "It is I, Saki."

Nar. "Oh, Saki, why did you come?"

Q. "I came for my bowl."

Nar. "Saki greetings, greetings, greetings, greetings, greetings, greetings, greetings, greetings, greetings.
Saki, what you all have done to me. A fine bowl is what you came for. Wọi has long ago let go of me and dropped me. You yourself were over that way long ago. You were doing that."

Respond to the song, respond to the song, my friend, respond.
Ee-oo, Wọi has let go of me and dropped me.

25. The sound of intercourse.

Ee-oo, Wọi has let go of me and dropped me.
Only the bowl's owner knows its price.
Bongkai kpolong, kpolong, kpolong, kpolong, kpolong, kpolong. Bongkai kpolong, kpolong, kpolong, kpolong fẹẹ laa. Koro, koro, mọnọ, mọnọ, fẹẹ laa.

Q. What is doing that?

Nar. Koro, koro, mọnọ, mọnọ, fẹẹ laa.
She is carving the bowl.
Koro, koro, mọnọ, mọnọ, fẹẹ laa.
Bowl flat, bowl large inside, bowl well-finished, well-finished.
Ee, Saki, that is your bowl, oh.
Oh, pass, let's go to bed.

Q. Oh, she has finished it.

Nar. It is Keapee whose bowl matter is still left here today.
Oh, it is Malong-yaa-pu who is pitiful.
It is Malong-yaa-pu who is pitiful.[26]

Aud. "Hello, woman."

Nar. "Who is this?"

Aud. "It is I, Keapee."

Nar. "Keapee, why did you come?"

Aud. "I came for a bowl."

Nar. "You long ago entered Wọi's ears, he has hated me here, I have come here. I am here so that different men come, and is that why you have come here?"
Kpitili, kpitili, thick bowl, don't come here again, ee.[27]

Q. Oh, have they finished Keapee's bowl?

Nar. Didn't you hear what she told her? She told her, "You long ago entered into Wọi's ears."
Ee-ee, Keapee, wee.
Ee, it is the car that brought me, ee.
A direct car brought me here, ee.
A direct car brought me here, ee.

Q. "Hello, woman."

---

26. Here the narrator indirectly comments on the situation of the jealous wife.

27. Here, in contrast, the carving of something for women is quick, and "kpitili" is the sound of something ugly and thick that has not been well worked.

Nar. "Who is that?"

Q. "It is I, Bena."

Nar. "Bena greetings, Bena greetings, Bena greetings, Bena greetings, Bena greetings, Bena greetings, Bena greetings. You came for what reason, my people?"

Q. "My bowl, I've been going with it and it has spoiled. That is why I've come for a new one."

Nar. "Oh, Bena, what you did to me is big, Bena."
One single, single bowl.
One single, single bowl.
Bongkai kpolong, kpolong, kpolong, kpolong, kpolong, kpolong, kpolong, kpolong, kpolong, kpolong, kpolong, kpolong, kpolong.
Flat, well-finished, well-finished, shiny black, shiny black, smooth.
Koro, koro, mọnọ, mọnọ, fẹẹ laa.
Bowl flat, bowl well-finished, well-finished, bowl shiny black, shiny black, bowl large inside, bowl well-finished, well-finished.
Bena, that's your bowl.
Oh, pass, let's go to the bed, oh.

Q. Thank you, for me.

Nar. Dried millet, wẹsẹ.

Ch. Wẹsẹ.

EPISODE 6

House Moves into Battle

Nar. Large, large Rooster, it's the fight going there, oh.
Ah-oh, large Rooster, oh, it's the fight going there, oh.[28]
Yes, it's the fight going, oh.
Large, large Rooster, oh.
Large, large Rooster, oh, large, it's the fight going, oh.

Ch. Large, large Rooster, large.

Nar. It's the fight going, large, large Rooster, oh.
It's the fight going there, oh.

---

28. The rooster takes the role of a praise singer, a musician who goes into battle with the warrior. The previous mention of rooster as the one who must dominate though hen's voice is sweeter serves further to characterize the praise singer.

Aa-ee.
I am telling you. That's right.

Q. My friend, from whose mouth is that song again? Don't lie to me, oh.

Nar. Ee, Maa-laa-ke-ma, oh.
Ee, Maa-laa-ke-ma, bring my voice, oh my people.
Oh-wee, Rooster-wee, the fight is going there.
Sun-falling, Maa-laa-ke-ma, it's the fight going there.
Sun-falling, Maa-laa-ke-ma, oh wee.
Sun-falling, Maa-laa-ke-ma, oh wee.
Mẹni-maa-fa is sitting in the forest.

Q. What thing's name is that now?

Nar. There's a male monster spirit and Wọi's vehicle has gone up. And, and Wọi, the Rooster sings the vehicle as it goes up.

Q. Oh, that's the voice of the Rooster.

Nar. That's the voice of the Rooster. The fight has gone, oh. I have never done any of it, ee. Ee, Rooster, oh, the fighting.
Oh, Maa-laa-ke-ma, oh, large Rooster, oh.
Wọi has gone, ee.
Sun-falling, sun that doesn't wait until noon.
Large Rooster, the fight is going.
Zi, zi, zi, zi, zi, zi, zi, zi, zi, zi, zi, zi, zi, zi.

Q. What thing's sound is that again?

Nar. The house's traveling sound that is.

Q. Oh-koo.

Nar. The house has risen into the distant sky. The house is going.

Q. Wọi's house?

Nar. Wọi's house.

Q. Were you near there?

Nar. Very close, really.
All the things were responding. I tell you the gboto frogs in the swamp were responding, "Wọi, wọi."[29] Do you know gboto's voice? There's the house they are announcing. Isn't it so?

Q. Oh.

---

29. As the battle heats up, this is reflected by more voices performing. The singing of frogs is prominent in Kpelle stories. Various kinds of frogs are typified as singing in various ways.

Nar. The gọọ frogs are responding. And Wọi.

Ee, Maa-laa-ke-ma-oo, ee-yee, it's the fight going there, oh.
The fight is going there, large, large Rooster.

Q. Is Wọi ready for his war?

Nar. Wọi is really ready for the war. Palm-nut-cutting-bunch-is-shaking has gone and stood in Wọi's path over there. And he isn't equal to Wọi. The house is going to Palm-nut-cutting-is-shaking's place.

Q. Oh, my friend.

Nar. Dried millet, wẹsẹ.

Ch. Wẹsẹ.

Nar. Yọọ yọọ.

EPISODE 7

House Meets Bẹlẹ-Tree

Nar. Ee, Maa-laa, bring my voice goa yeng yeng,
Goa Zu-kpeei bilang, oh.

Ch. Goa yeng yeng yeng, goa yeng.

S.S. Zu-kpeei bilang, oh.

Nar. Zou, zou, zou, zou, zou, zou, zou, zou.

Aud. What is doing that?

Nar. Zou, zou, zou, zou, zou.
Because they argued with me.

Aud. My friend, what is that again doing that?

Nar. Ee, Maa-laa-ke-ma, oh goa Zu-kpeei bilang, oh.
Goa yeng, yeng, yeng, goa Zu-kpeei bilang, oh.

Aud. Kulung, don't lie to me here!

Nar. Why should I lie to you? What do you say, what do you say?
Eh, Wọi came, Wọi just came. The bees that were long ago on the cow's horn left and poured into a Bẹlẹ-Tree. The bees produced an enormous amount of honey. The bees were on the Bẹlẹ-Tree.[30] A very large Bẹlẹ-Tree. A very large

30. Here the bees that earlier were on the cow's horns have descended to the tree, a thread that economically, though not causally, links the two segments.

Bẹlẹ-Tree and, and Wọi has remained in the sky. He said to his child Zu-kpeei, he said to him, "That's fine. Chop down the Bẹlẹ-Tree and take out the honey. Let's eat the honey before we go to fight the war."

Aud. Is he speaking the truth?

Nar. My friend!

Aud. Don't lie to me, oh.

Q. What is this person's name?

Nar. Wọi-boi, Wọi-boi, Wọi is in the distant sky.
Wọi's child is Zu-kpeei.[31]

Q. Zu-kpeei.

Nar. Zu-kpeei's younger sibling is Wọi-boi. He said, "Chop the Bẹlẹ-Tree."

Q. Yes, of the two people, who is cutting the Bẹlẹ-Tree?

Nar. Zu-kpeei and Wọi-boi in addition to Maa-pu.
Maa-pu, then, is sitting over there. She is a woman.
She is a very important ritual specialist. She passes gas and a fire breaks out.

Q. Who is passing gas, who is cutting the tree?

Nar. Zu-kpeei is cutting the tree, and Wọi-boi.
My fellow, the questions you are asking are big.

Q. I want to understand it.

Nar. Ee, Zu-kpeei, goa Zu-kpeei bilang, oh.
Goa yeng, yeng, yeng, Zu-kpeei bilang, oh.
Zou, zou, zou, zou.

Q. Is that the sound of cutting the tree?

Nar. Mm, ah. They are cutting the tree I tell you.
One string of thread it was he put around his waist.
He put sticks into it and stood on them. They stood there.
Wọi-boi stood thus, Zu-kpeei stood thus.
They are cutting the Bẹlẹ-Tree. The Bẹlẹ-Tree is large and a Male-Lizard is in the crown of the Bẹlẹ.

Q. What will it do?

---

31. Here we get some explanation of Wọi's family relationships which are generally understood and not defined in detail.

Nar. Ee, Maa-laa-ke-ma, oh.
Aa-oi-yo, goa Zu-kpeei bilang, oh.
Yeng, yeng, yeng goa Zu-kpeei bilang, oh.
Yeng, yeng, yeng goa Zu-kpeei bilang, oh.
Yeng, yeng, yeng goa Zu-kpeei bilang, oh.
Zou, zou, zou, zou, ze-zou, zou, zou.

You yourself, the age of Western axes. You yourself, a person is cutting trees with a young man's style. Even if a person is old, he shows off and does his things.

Aud. Will he fell it?

Q. Well, will they fell it?

Nar. The tree will do what to fall? Oh, the Bẹlẹ they are chopping, I tell you. A Male-Lizard is there at the fork of the Bẹlẹ, there is no approaching.

Aud. What will he do?

Nar. Ee, Maa-laa bring my voice.
Kpoo, ee Zu-kpeei bilang, oh.
Yeng, yeng, yeng, goa Zu-kpeei bilang, oh.
Yeng, yeng, yeng, goa Zu-kpeei bilang, oh.
Yeng, yeng, yeng, goa Zu-kpeei bilang, oh.

Q. I want to ask you.

Nar. Ask me.

Q. The song that they are singing, the two people chopping the tree, who is singing that song?

Nar. Ah, Maa-pu is skyward. Maa-pu is sitting there so that when the tree falls, she will start a fire on her buttocks.

Q. Yes.

Nar. Maa-pu, that's Zu-kpeei's sister they call Maa-pu.
And she starts a fire. She just speaks and it starts.
When she passes gas, it ignites.

Q. Oh!

Nar. All right, she is sitting over there waiting for the tree to fall. And the Male-Lizard, the monster spirit from the forest they call Mẹni-maa-fa, that's the Male-Lizard. They girdled the tree, and the Male-Lizard came out "kala, kala, kala." He hit his head on the scar "kpoo" and the tree was restored.

Q. The tree was restored?

Nar. It was restored.

Q. Then will they cut it down today?

Nar.
Keapee see me, Keapee see me, Keapee see me, Keapee see me, Keapee see me, Keapee see me, Keapee see me.
Ee, Zu-kpeei bilang-oo.

Respond to the song, oh, respond to the song, oh. Don't spoil my reputation here, oh.

Aud. Don't lie to me. They say you lie.

Nar. When I have been in Yilataa, when I have been in Yilataa, have I ever lied to you? When I have been in Yilataa, have I ever lied to you when performing epic there?

Oh, goa Zu-kpeei bilang, oh.
Oh, goa Zu-kpeei bilang, oh.

Zu-kpeei has gone into the distant sky. He said, "Wọi."
He said to him, "Ee."
He said, "There is something at the fork of the tree."
He said, "What thing is there?"
He said, "There is a Male-Lizard there."
He said, "Is that correct?"
He said, "Mm."
He said to him, "Then let me give you something to go with you."

Aud. They say you are a liar.

Nar. Very close.

Aud. So.

Nar.
He said, "Is that right?"
He said, "Mm."
He said, "Because we just cut the Bẹlẹ-Tree and when it is about to fall, a Male-Lizard at the fork of the tree comes and hits the fork, his head restores the cut."

Q. What will they do with the Lizard?

Nar. Zu-kpeei opened his box. There was a Bow in there in addition to an Arrow.

Q. What will he do with the Bow and Arrow?

Nar.
He said, "Bow, you and I met for what?"
He said, "When a problem comes to you, I will help you."
He said, "That's fine."
"You and these people go, that Lizard humbugging, or so, you, Bow, I want to see that lizard in your hand."

That's the Bow. You yourself, all those things were talking.

Q. Yes.

Nar. The Bow has talked, the Arrow has talked. All have songs.
I'll come there.
Dried millet, węsę.

Ch. Węsę

Nar. Am I doing it?

Aud. You are doing it well.

Q. You are trying.

Nar. Is that right? I told you four days.

Aud. What were you doing with it?

Nar. We were doing it. Man, give me my beer.

Aud. Yours is there.

Nar. You have drunk yours and you say this? Stop, a person doesn't do things like that.

Q. This Bow that is talking with its owner, I want to hear its song.

Nar. Isn't this mine?

Q. You should just be concerned to sing songs. Yours is inside it.

Nar. Leave mine in the bottle.

Q. My ear is on the song they are coming to go with.

Nar. But I did not stop Zu-kpeei's song, oh. I didn't stop it. But it is what the Bow will enter with because when the Male-Lizard comes out of the sky and comes down, then the Bow is now ready.

Aud. Yes.

EPISODE 8

Lizard is Struck. Bęlę-Tree Becomes House

Nar. Ee-oh, ee-oh, I want to make an Iron-Bow, iron what?
Make an Iron-Bow.
Make an Iron-Bow.

Aud. Make an Iron-Bow, raise it.

Ch. Ee, ee, ee, ee.
Oh, make an Iron-Bow, oh-ee.

Nar. Oh, I want to make an Iron-Bow, oh-ee.
Wọi has given me an Iron-Bow.
Wọi has given me an Iron-Bow.
Oh, Maa-laa, bring my voice.
Sun-falling, they are calling us again at night.[32]
Ee-oh, the St. Paul wasn't deep at night.[33]
My fellow, can't you seat that muu on it?[34]

Q. I can raise the muu, but I want to hear the song words very well.

Nar. That's the song from the mouth of Bow. Bow in addition to Arrow.

Q. Is that the song from their mouths?

Nar. It is the song from their mouths.
That Male-Lizard in the sky that comes and knocks its head on the scar and the Bẹlẹ-Tree is one. Wọi made the Male-Lizard and gave it to Zu-kpeei and Maa-pu.[35] In order for them to have that bow. It will take the Male-Lizard out of the tree.

Q. Are the Iron-Bow and Arrow singing the song?

Nar. Eh?

Q. Are the Iron-Bow and Arrow singing the song?

Nar. The Iron-Bow?
Give me the Arrow.
Give me the Arrow.
Give me the Arrow.
Give me the Arrow.
Give me the Arrow.
Give me the Arrow.
Give me the Arrow.
Give me the Arrow.
That song is coming, but what is bringing it? Is Wọi bringing it? We don't know. But the song is coming after those proverbs.

Q. That's what I want to hear.

---

32. The singer implies that he is obliged to perform extensively not only a day's worth of work but a night's as well.

33. There was a singer, Siafa-tolong, who crossed the St. Paul River with his lover at night by walking on water. They needed no boat. This single phrase recalls a well-known legend. It also refers to the power that Wọi possesses to accomplish supernatural acts.

34. The *muu* is a low-pitched ostinato pattern that regularly is added to enhance the chorus part. Here the narrator wants it added to the ensemble performance.

35. By agreement of all I interviewed, the narrator errs here and should not have mentioned the male lizard when he was, in fact, referring to the bow and arrow.

Nar. I don't take out the head, oh. I told you, let's go, oh. A person doesn't take the head out of an epic.

Q. I understand.

Nar.

Oh, Maa-laa, bring my voice.
Eh, Maa-laa, bring my voice, oh.
Oh, I want to make an Iron-Bow, oh-ya.
Oh, I want to make an Iron-Bow, oh-ya.
Oh, I want to make an Iron-Bow, oh-ya.
A foolish dancer doesn't know a bad place, oh-ya.
A foolish dancer doesn't know a bad place, oh-ya.
Eh, song catcher, oh.

They said to the women, "Go up, let's go up to the farm quickly."
Wọi said, "Go to the farm quickly." And they have gone there.

Zou, zou, zou, zou, zou, zou.
I'm mixing it, oh.
I'm mixing it, ah.

Q. Then what happened, the Male-Lizard came out of the house and was coming?

Nar.

Zou, zou, zou, zou, zou.

The Male-Lizard stretched "ngoro" and was coming.
The Bow is really ready. You yourself, the Bow is a person, oh.

Q. Yes.

Nar.

That's the song.
Ee-eh, I want to make an Iron-Bow, oh.
Oh, I want to make an Iron-Bow.
Sun-falling, I want to make an Iron-Bow.
Maa-laa-kẹ, oh, I want to make an Iron-Bow, eh.
Sun-falling, I want to make an Iron-Bow.
That's the song.
That's the song.
That's the song.
That's the song.

The people just spoke and the Male-Lizard came out and started talking. You yourself, Bow. You know Bow.
Life is inside of it.
It hit "kpe" and it turned. Bow. Zu-kpeei made it and Wọi.

But by itself, Bow hit it there. But you yourself, Wọi fixes everything with his voice.[36]

Aud. Oh.

Nar. He said, "This thing is a person." He used it. My people, don't you hear my words?

Q. You are saying it for us to really understand the point.

Nar. Wọi did things with just his mouth, with his voice. If he said a person should die, that one died. But, then, he doesn't do that because he is a chief.

Ee-eh, I want to make an Iron-Bow, oh-ya.
Sun-falling, I want to make an Iron-Bow, oh-ya.
Oh, Gbangsu Bono, bring my voice, oh my people.
Ee, Maa-laa-ke-ma, bring my voice, oh my people.
Oh, a foolish dancer doesn't know an ugly place.
You see him like an old male chimpanzee.
Bang, bang, bang, bang, bang, bang, bang, bang,
bang, bang, bang, bang, bang, bang, bang, bang.

When he hit it, the Male-Lizard, I tell you, he came out and fell flat.

Q. Has he died now?

Nar. Because, that Bẹlẹ-Tree, it is the Bẹlẹ-Tree doing the thing. The Bẹlẹ has flown, it didn't fall.

Q. Eh?

Nar. The Bẹlẹ has flown and become one of Wọi's houses.

Dried millet, wẹsẹ.

Ch. Wẹsẹ.

EPISODE 9

House Moves

Nar.

Dua kpenee.
Ee, I'm going to Zu-kpeei, dua kpenee.
Dua kpenee.

Respond to the song. Stop, let me tell you, eh. My in-law, don't shame me here.

Aud. No one should shame him.

---

36. This is another reference to power, often supernatural, of the human voice. The voice carries weight to accomplish much and defeat many.

Nar. Ah-ah. They are raising the song. Ah-ah, respond well to the song. Let me show it to you.

That Bẹlẹ-Tree, the Bẹlẹ didn't fall. All the people have remained on the Bẹlẹ-Tree, they have gone into the distant sky. They are going to fight. That is the song for it. That is the Bẹlẹ-traveling-song.

Aud. Yes.

Nar. The Bẹlẹ is the house. That's its traveling song.
This is it I'm showing it to you. My friend, I'm telling you, sing it so that Keapee hears it well. So she doesn't say this man lies. Do you hear? You all are God's speakers . . .

Aud. Raise that one.

Nar. Dua kpenee.

Stop, stop let me show it to you. Wait, lay the kọne down.

Dua kpenee.
I'm going to Zu-kpeei's place, dua kpenee.
Dua kang kalong, ah-eh-re.
Dua kpenee, eh-eh-eh dua.

Ch. Eh, eh-re.

Nar. Answer as one. Raise the muu together. Complete the second. Eh, it's not this voice. That is just this person's part.

Ch. Eh-eh-re, dua kpenee.
Dua kang kalong, ah-eh-re, dua kpenee.
Dua kang kalong, ah-eh-re.
Dua kang kalong, ah-eh-re.
Dua kang kalong, ah-eh-re.
Dua kang kalong, ah-eh-re.
Dua kang kalong, ah-eh-re.

Nar. Ah, no, that's the song, oh. That is the song by which we will travel. We will travel with songs grouped on it, but stay with it.[37]
Dried millet, wẹsẹ

Dua kpenee, I'm going to Zu-kpeei, dua kpenee.
Dua kang kalong ah-eh-re.
Ah-oh, a house is not the neck [roof].
Dua kang kalong ah-eh-re.
Dua kpenee.

37. The ending of Episode Nine and the beginning of Episode Ten are blurred because of the use of the same background song. Since the audience expects a new song, Kulung goes to some lengths to explain why he can use the song without violating expectations.

That's yours.

Ch. Dua kpenee.
Dua kang kalong ah-eh-re.
Dua kang kalong ah-eh-re.

Nar. I'm going to Zu-kpeei, dua kpenee.
My friend, wait for me, don't take it fast, fast.
Dua kpenee.
Dua kpenee.
Dua kpenee.
Eh, Maa-laa-ke-ma, oh, a house is not its neck.

Q. I want to see you and ask you.

Nar. We are again inside the distant sky.

Q. What will happen again?

Nar. But that is the song. Yes, that is a fine song. And you say the song isn't fine?

Q. What will happen?

Nar. Eh, Goli-kping-kpa bring my voice.
Eh, Maa-laa, oh, dua kpenee.
Eh, Maa-laa-ke-ma, oh.
Ah-eh, a house is not its neck.
Sun-falling, falling, falling.
Eh, I'm going to Maa-pu, dua kpenee.
Ah-mm, a dancer doesn't simply stand outside.
Gono-wee, catch the song.
Then she has broken the law of the dance.
Ah, Sun-under-the-brush, what did you say to me?
Ah-oh, Snuff-lover-wee, dua kpenee.
Sun-falling, falling.
Eh, I'm going to Lẹẹ-tii.
That's the house traveling song.

Q. My friend, is the house going again?

Nar. The house is inside the distant sky and is traveling.
All the people are inside the house. You yourself are in the house.

Q. Me?

Nar. You. Your picture is there.
Zi, zi, zi, zi, zi, zi.
[Tape runs out here. Ending cue is given.]

EPISODE 10

House Arrives at Koing-Tree

Nar. Dua kpenee.
Dua kang kalong ah-eh-re.
That's a fine song, man.

Ch. Dua kpenee.
Dua kang kalong, ah-eh-re.
Dua kpenee.

Nar. Wait, wait.
Dua kpenee.
Wait. Let me show you.
Dua kpenee.
I'm going to Zu-kpeei's place, dua kpenee.

Ch. Dua kang kalong, ah-eh-re.

Nar. Eh, you pull it a little. But if you cut it short like that, it's not good. Wait.
Dua kpenee.
Dua kpenee.
Listen to me. Wait.
Dua kpenee.
Ee, dua kpenee.
That's yours.
They reward the song catcher because of her fine voice.
Ah-ee, dua kpenee.
Take it.
Ee-oh, a house is not its neck.
Sun-falling-ee, I'm going to Zu-kpeei's place, dua kpenee.
Oh my people, come Maa-laa, my people.
To Maa-pu's place, dua kpenee.
Maa-wee, the tomo song.
Maa-wee, dua kpenee.
Mm, Sun-falling, "kpoo."

Q. Where is this house going?

Nar. The house is going up.
Zi, zi, zi, zi, zi, zi, zi.
It is the house that the battle is following.
Zi, zi, zi.

Q. Where did you say that the house is going?

Nar. The house is really going up. It goes on the ocean [America] and comes from there . . .

Q. What place is up?

Nar. Epic, don't you know? I tell you they don't take the head out of an epic. Don't you know, my friend?

Q. Eh-eh, but up is what I want to know.

Nar. Ah, it's going into the sky.
Respond to the song. That's the song.
Ee, Maa-laa-ke-ma, "kpoo."
Folo-too-too, oh.
Eh, I'm going to Maa-laa's place, dua kpenee.
Folo-too, oh, folo-too.
Oh, a house is not its neck, dua kpenee.
It was Męni-maa-fa long ago. Męni-maa-fa is running underneath the house fast. Really, really, "kili, kili, kili." It came to the bottom of a Koing-Tree.

Q. It came to what?

Nar. Base of a Koing-Tree.

Q. Base of a Koing-Tree?

Nar. Base of a Koing-Tree. And Wọi's sister was in Męni-maa-fa's hand. He said, "Then that is a good matter." He said, "This is Wọi who has raised his house into the sky. His wife that he had, that is she who has come."
I tell you that the head of an epic doesn't come out. But all of you know it.
Base of a Koing-Tree. Koing.
Koing, Koing that our old people cut for a door.
They carved it and put it at the doorway of the house.
Koing.
That's the song, man. Wake up. Clap your hands, man.
All of you, all of you, all of you.
The epic has gotten down.
Eh, Maa-laa-ke-ma, oh my people.
Sun-falling tomo, oh, oh.
I'm going to Maa-pu's place my people, dua kpenee.
Eh, Maa-laa-ke-ma, bring my voice, my people.
Ah-oh, a house is not the neck, dua kpenee.
Mm-mm, oh-oh.
Eh, Beads-over-the-pants, dua kpenee.
Oh my people, Zu-kpeei, my friend, bring my voice.

Ee-oh, dua kpenee.
Oh people, my friend, friend, friend, friend, oh-koo.
Dua kpenee.
Oh my friend, my friend, bring my voice, my friend, my friend.
Oh-koo, dua kpenee.
Zi, zi-zi, zi, zi.

The house is going to the base of the Koing-Tree.

Q. Oh, my friend, what is he going to do with it?

Nar. Zi, zi, zi, zi, zi.

Mẹni-maa-fa is going. He said to him, "Base-of-the-Koing."
He said, "Mm."
He said, "Why did we meet?"
He said, "We met so that if a difficult matter comes to you I can help. This is Wọi, his wife's name is Gele-ngoi, he has taken her from me. He is in his vehicle, he is coming thus. If he comes, he shouldn't pass here."

Q. What can Koing-Tree and fellows do?

Nar. Oh, it has hit it, it has hit it, "pu." The base of the Koing-Tree has scattered, scattered, it has risen and entered the sky. It has come down across the sea.

But I tell you, I'm pourer of epic. We have come to tell it, oh.

Q. So that the house doesn't pass.

Nar. The house shouldn't pass.

Aud. Don't lie to me, oh.

Q. What will Wọi do again to pass?

Nar. Just sit, you will see me.

I'm going to Maa-pu, dua kpenee.
Ee, Maa-pu, wee.
Sun-falling, a house is not its neck, dua kpenee.
Ee, Maa-laa-kẹ-ma, bring my voice.
Zi-pilii, put on the neck, oh ya.
Sun-falling.
Ee, Maa-laa-kẹ-ma, oh dua kpenee.
Zi, zi, zi, zi, zi-zi, zi, zi-zi, zi, zi-zi, zi, zi-zi.

The house is going. It is going to the Koing. It is going to the Koing. It is not far yet. The distance just remains thus.

Nyee-pu, look at me, Nyee-pu, look at me, Nyee-pu, look at me.

The house is really going, I tell you, to the base of the Koing, really on the base of the Koing. It sits on the Koing "kpi."

Aud. Oh.

Nar. Eh-eh. He said to him, "How is it?"
He said, "They say you shouldn't pass here."
He said, "I, did you speak to me?"
He said, "Mm."
He said, "You are a tree and you speak to me?"
He said, "Mm."
He said, "That's a good matter." He hit his bag here.
He said, "Who is here?"
Axe said, "It is I."
He said, "Who is here?"
Cutlass said, "It is I."
He said, "Why did we meet?"
He said, "We met so that if a difficult matter falls on you I can help."
He said, "Then get down here. Cut the base of the Koing so the house can pass."

Q. The Cutlass and the wise Axe, they can cut the large base of the Koing-Tree how?

Nar. They have come to cut it quickly.

Q. Except they cut it and I see.

Nar. Ee, Maa-laa-ke-ma, bring my voice, oh my people.
Ee, Maa-laa-ke-ma, oh ee-re, dua kpenee.
I am going to Work-left's place, dua kpenee.

Dried millet, wẹsẹ

EPISODE 11

Cutlass and Axe Chop Koing-Tree

Nar. Vangee, Vangee, I am Vangee.
Vangee, Vangee, I am Vangee.
Vangee, Vangee, I am Vangee.

Ch. Vangee, Vangee.
Mm-mm, Vangee, Vangee.

Nar. I am Vangee.

That's yours.

Ch. I am Vangee.
Vangee, Vangee.

Nar. I am Vangee, Vangee, Vangee.
I am Vangee, oh.
Oh, the voice from there is sweet.
And I cut it.

Q. That is the song from whose mouth?

Nar. Kpakila, Kpakila didn't cross the water before Alligator caught him.

Q. Is that the voice of the Axe and Cutlass?

Nar. That's their song.
Ee, Goli-kping-gba, I am Vangee.
Kpakila didn't cross the water before Alligator caught him.
Geu, geu, balau.

Q. What have they done?

Nar. It cuts it, it splits it. He said, "I cut it and split it."

Q. Oh, my friend. Let them cut the base of the Koing-Tree and I see.

Nar. Don't forget, oh,
Don't forget, oh,
Don't forget, oh,
Don't forget, oh,
Don't forget, oh.
Vangee, Vangee, I am Vangee.

Yes.

Vangee, Vangee, I am Vangee.
The voice from there is sweet for me.
I am the one who cut it.
Oh, my people, a young woman's voice is sweet for me.
I'm the one who cut it.
Sun-falling, ee, I'm the one who cut it.
Sun-falling, I'm the one who cut it.
Geu, geu, balau, geu, geu, balau, gau, gau, gau, balau.

Q. Oh, my friend.

Nar. Keep explaining it to Keapee.

Q. I say, is it the Cutlass that cuts it and the Axe that splits it?

Nar. Cutlass and Axe. The Cutlass cuts it and the Axe splits it. He's the one doing it there. He will finish right now and the vehicle will again go up.

Q. Go up into the sky?

Nar. It goes again into the sky. It travels and fights the war. Palm-nut-cutting-the-shoot-shaking and all of them have fled and gone to meet the vehicle.

Ee, I am Vangee, oh.
Vangee, Vangee, I am Vangee.
The voice from there is sweet for me.
I am the one who cuts it.
Ah, my people, Kpakila didn't cross the water before
Alligator caught him.
Eh, Maa-laa, bring my voice, oh.
Ah-oo, I am Vangee.
Oh, I am Vangee.

The vehicle is setting, the vehicle is turning, it goes back, it comes. You yourself, you yourself, don't you know the vehicles, the big vehicles that rise from Robert's Field and go up into the sky?

Wọi's vehicle.[38]

Ee-oh, it is Vangee, oh.
Ee-oh, it is Vangee, Vangee, Vangee, oh.
Oh, the voice from there is sweet for me.
I'm the one who cuts it.
The voice from there is sweet for me.
I'm the one who cuts it.

That's the voice of the Cutlass, oh. The Cutlass says, "The voice from there is sweet for me." It says, "A young woman's voice is sweet for me." "I'm the one who cuts it." It is on his mind.

The Axe says, "If you cut it, I split it." Eh, that's the voice of the Axe. Axe says, "If you cut it, I split it." That's the voice of the Axe. Axe says, "If you cut it, I split it." That's a huge Cutlass. It is cutting the roots of the Koing-Tree.

Gbo, gbo, gbo, gbo, gbo, gbo.

The Axe was coming there.

Balau, balau, balau.

The house is standing and going "zige-zige" I tell you.

Ah-ee, I'm Vangee.
Vangee, Vangee, I'm Vangee.
Sun, bird, ah-oh, Vangee.
Ee, Maa-laa-kẹ-ma, oh.

38. Here a modern adaptation occurs as the house becomes a vehicle identified as a plane. Note that the sound and rhythm of movement have not changed.

Ee, Bird-wee, Vangee.
Mm, Tomo-yoo, I'm Vangee.
Kpakila didn't cross the water before Alligator caught him.
My friends, let's respond underneath it.
Ah-oh, Left-work, where are you going?
My friends, let's respond underneath it, oh.
Ah-oh, Left-work, where are you going?
My friends, it's embarrassment.
My friends, it's embarrassment.
Ah-oh, Left-work, where are you going?
Ah, my people, my friend, my friend, Maa-laa-kẹ-ma.
Know-oh, I am going.
Oh, my people, my friend, Keapee, I am going.
Mm, say it.
Gbou, gbou, gbou, gbou, balau, gbou, gbou, gbou, balau, gbou, gbou, balau.

Q. But the Cutlass doesn't fool around, oh.

Nar. Gbou, balau.
The Rooster whose song I started, it's the Rooster who announces for Wọi. All the base has broken, I tell you. The house has gotten up, the house is going. Mẹni-maa-fa has again passed there, "fili," and is going. He wants Wọi's sister they call Gele-ngoi, he wants to take her by force, but he isn't equal to Wọi. He throws the sword and says to him, "Come, go back. Get down on your owner's feet." He broke his foot.

Q. Oh, my friend.

Nar. Ah, my people, I didn't say it all, that's it. To stop is what? Of course he wants to take the woman from his in-law, but he is not able. And Wọi is a ritual specialist.

Q. And he isn't able to beat him.

Nar. He isn't able to beat Wọi. Well, the house is in the sky.
Ee, Golii, bring my voice.
He came to Bat.

Q. My friend, what thing?

Nar. Mẹni-maa-fa.

Q. What is he coming to do again?

Nar. He has met Bat. He said to him, "Bat."
He said, "Ee?"

He said, "Wọi has taken my woman from me."
He said, "Is that right?"
He said, "Mm."
He said, "What should I do?"
He said, "He has taken my woman, don't let him pass here.
That is the house in the sky. It is coming."
Bat said, "Then it is a good matter. Oh, if it is so, well, Wọi?"
He said, "Mm."
"And Zu-kpeei?"
He said, "Mm."
He said, "They are not equal to me one bit."

Aud. Is that Bat's voice?

Nar. That is Bat's voice.

Aud. What can that clever bat do?

Nar. Dried millet, wẹsẹ.

Ch. Wẹsẹ.

EPISODE 12

Bat Assaults House and Is Caught

Nar. Ee, Bat, oh, kpa yereng, yereng, yereng, ee.

Ch. Kpa yereng, Bat, yereng, ee.

Nar. Bat, yereng, ee.
That's yours.
Bat, oh.
Don't respond with a bad voice.

Ch. Bat, oh.
My voice is not bad.

Nar. Ee, ee, ee. You yourself, do you know Bat? Ee, this is Bat.
Ah-oh, Bat, oh.
Bat, do you know Bat? When evening falls, it passes thus.
When it comes out from underneath the eaves, it can sharpen a knife, I tell you. So that when Zu-kpeei comes, when the house comes, it would break the house.

Q. My friend, what can Bat do?

Nar. My friend, respond, man. That's a really fine song.
Kpa yereng, yereng, yereng, ee kpa yereng.
Kpa yereng, yereng, yereng, ee kpa yereng.
Maa-pu, this is Zu-kpeei's knife, no one takes it by force.

Maa-pu, this is Zu-kpeei's knife, no one takes it by force.
Ee, Bat, bring my voice.

Bat is really passing. He is passing in the night, he is passing in the night. He is passing in the night.
Wọi hit his bag. He said, "Who is here?"
He said, "It is I."
He said, "You, what is your name?"
He said, "My name is Dried-koong-leaf."
He said, "Why did we meet?"
He said, "We met so that when a difficult matter comes to you, I can do something to help." He said, "Then get down here."

Q. What?

Nar. Dried-koong-leaf. Dried-koong-leaf has gotten out of the bag.

Q. What will he do with Bat?

Nar. He will catch it within.

Q. The Bat that was sharpening the knife?

Nar. So, what has it done with the knife?

He is sparring "vang, vang, vang, vang, vang, vang, vang, vang, vang."

Wọi put his hand in here, Dried-koong-leaf went "fang." Bat is passing, you yourself. He was passing, passing thus, "via, via, via, via, via." He just showed Dried-koong-leaf and he came and entered into it. He went into the bag.

Q. Has he caught that war?

Nar. He has caught that war. The vehicle is going.

Yọọ-yọọ.
Dried millet, wẹsẹ.
That's the vehicle driving song, that's just the one song we drive the vehicle with and go. We are going and doing things and coming back.

Ch. Yes.

Nar. Do you understand? Because that is the way the man long ago told me. So that they don't say that I sing one song over and over. I know you remember the songs I've been singing.

Q. We understand it.

Nar. Ee-ee. That vehicle driving song, the vehicle is going up. Do you understand? Ee-ee, in the sky. That's its song, "Dua Kpenee." When we go to Mẹni-maa-fa's place, they will fight the war. They fight the war, the war spoils on this person. We pass. The vehicle was in the sky and we were going. That's the song, "Dua Kpenee." Of all the songs, that is the head. So that you don't say that I can't perform epic, that I'm performing one episode twice. That's what I am telling you. Do you hear my voice, my friend? Ee-ee, driving the vehicle, that's the way the man long ago told me. The man's name was Singer. He long ago performed an epic for a day like I am doing it here for a day. I know it will remain in someone's memory so that he can perform it here. But if it doesn't remain in his memory, they will call me every day.

EPISODE 13

Pumpkin Is Placed to Block House

Nar. Dua kpenee.
Dua kpenee.
Explain it to Nyee-pu.
Dua kpenee.
Keapee, that's the vehicle moving song. That's the song I'm carrying, passing, taking small, small songs out of it. Do you understand? I sing it, passing and taking small, small songs from it. That song doesn't end. The vehicle is going up, but it doesn't reach there. My kneecap is really hurting. That's a fine song. Stop, respond well, man.

Ch. We are responding.

Nar. Ee, Maa-laa-kẹ-ma, dua kpenee.
Oh-ee, I'm going to Maa-laa's place, dua kpenee.
Sun-falling, falling, falling.
A house is not its neck, dua kpenee.
Wọi said, "That is a good matter." The vehicle is really moving. The vehicle has arisen and is going up.
It was that man who told me that long ago. If it is not so, then let the sun kill me. I do not lie.

Aud. Let it be from you.

Nar. The man long ago told me that. I myself was not born with it, but I heard it from a person in Beengla. They call the man Singer.
The way the man told it to me, that's the way I perform. And I do not lie.

Q. Has the house gotten up?

Nar. Zi, zi, zi, the house has gotten up.
Zi, zi, zi, zi, zi, zi-zi.
Everything is inside the house.

Aud. Oh.

Nar. Ee, Maa-laa-kẹ-ma, oh, ee-ya.
Dried millet, wẹsẹ.

Ch. Wẹsẹ.

Nar. Let's sing the song with our small voice and see. Let's sing it with our small voice. All of our voices are big.

Aud. Let another one begin.

Nar. Eh-eh. It's not different. It's the same song. I tell you, that's the house walking song.

Q. The house hasn't yet reached anything.

Nar. When the house reaches something, the thing will talk. The house and it will fight and the house will pass. It comes again to something. My in-law, the epic I tell in Yilataa, have you done it? Let's carry it.

Dua kpenee.
Ee, dua kpenee.

Eh-eh, that's the song.

Ch. Dua kpenee.
Dua kang kalo aa-ee-re.

Nar. A house is not its neck, dua kpenee.
Ah-oo, I'm going to Maa-pu's place, dua kpenee.
Mm-mm, my friend, Mei-woo, dua kpenee.
Sunshine.

Mẹni-ma-faa has really passed, Mẹni-ma-faa has really passed. "Pala, pala, pala, pala." He is thinking that something is fighting Wọi but is not equal to Wọi.

Q. Where is he going again?

Nar. He has come to a whole pumpkin. A complete pumpkin, huge like those on the farm.

Q. What is Pumpkin's fame?

Nar. You yourself know Pumpkin. It is a witch. Pumpkin is a witch. You yourself, don't you see, when a person swears on it, it kills him.

Q. Yes.

Nar. He said to him, "Pumpkin, I have come to you."
He said, "Why?"

He said, "Eh, my wife is in Wọi's house. And so I came to you for you to give me help in order . . ."
He said, "Mm."
He said, "My hand is underneath it."
He said, "Then what are you giving me?"
He said, "Fight the war first."
Pumpkin said, "That is a good matter. Let me swell."

Q. What should Pumpkin do?

Nar. It should puff up and strike the distant sky and come down on the ocean. Come down here.

Q. That clever Pumpkin?

Nar. Pumpkin. Don't you know they eat it as an oath and it kills people?

Q. I know.

Nar. It puffed up and landed on the distant sky, it landed here, it rose into the sky. There is no passageway for anything at all. The house was coming.

Q. But the house will not pass him.

Nar. Well.
Gonong-ee.
Ee-eh, a house is not its neck, dua kpenee.
Mm-mm, I'm going to Zu-kpeei's place, dua kpenee.
Ee, my friend, my friend, ee-ee-ee.
Ee, a house is not its neck, dua kpenee.
Sun-falling, oh.
Ee-oh, eh, Bird-wee, dua kpenee.
Wọi is approaching the Pumpkin.
Zi, zi, zi, zi.
The house is just like that airplane that brings all the loads from across the ocean.
Gerei goong, oh.
Ee-eh, a house is not it's neck, oh dua kpenee.
Ee-oh, I'm going to Maa-laa's place, dua kpenee.

Q. I say it is not going to pass the Pumpkin.

Nar. Oh, my people, a foolish dancer in a crowd doesn't know anything ugly.
I'm going to Maa-laa, dua kpenee.
Oh, people, my friend, my friend, bring my voice.
Eh, Beads-on-the-pants, dua kpenee.

Sun-falling, oh.
Ee, my friend, oh dua kpenee.
The house is going.
Zi, zi, zi.
Gonong ee gere nga, eh.

Q. Then is that the song that they have seen the Pumpkin?

Nar. Eh, the Pumpkin is splattering in the sky. I tell you, they have really seen it, I tell you. The house sat on it "kpi." The house has drawn back.

Q. How will he do it?

Nar. He said, "Oh." Wọi hit here.

Q. What will he do?

Nar. He hit the bag. "Why did we meet?" He said, "If a difficult matter comes to you, I can help you."
He said, "Then get down and look here."

Q. What is he taking out of there, the pouch?

Nar. Mm, dried millet, wẹsẹ.

Ch. Wẹsẹ.

EPISODE 14

Knife Cuts Pumpkin

Nar. Zo wọi wọi wee, and I've split the Pumpkin.
I am going.
Zo wọi, zo wọi wọi wee.
And I've split the Pumpkin, I'm going.

Ch. Zo wọi wọi wee.
Zo wọi wọi wule.

Nar. That's the voice of Wọi's Knife. He said, "I have split the Pumpkin and passed here."
Dried millet, wẹsẹ.
My friend, that is not the song.
Zo wọi wọi wule.
Zo wọi.
Zo wọi wọi wule.
My friends, I have split the Pumpkin and am going.

Ch. Zo wọi wọi wule.
Zo wọi.

Nar. You yourself, the Knife is double-edged.
You are singing it badly. No, I'm going to stop that song, man.
Dried millet, wẹsẹ.

EPISODE 15

Poling Fights Gemila

Nar. Poling is fine, eh, dameyaa, dameyaa.
Poling is fine, eh, dameyaa, dameyaa.
Dameyaa, dameyaa, Poling is fine, eh.
That's the song.

Q. Whose song is that?

Nar. That is Poling's song.
Poling has come to do all, to fight war. One man they call Gemila, he is powerful. And so they called Poling to his feast so that she could come and defeat him.

Aud. Oh.

Nar. Gemila is powerful, when he fells someone, he plucks out the eye.

Q. Really?

Nar. Very close.
My friend, Maa-laa, bring my voice.
Ee, Maa-laa.
My knees have really gotten sore.
Ee, Maa-laa, bring my voice.
There is Poling with the carved beads on it.
There is Poling with the carved beads on it.
There is Poling with the carved beads on it.
There is Poling with the carved beads on it.
Gemila is really powerful, he really beats people.
He takes out their eyeballs. But Poling is not powerful, but she is smart. Poling is not powerful.

Aud. I know.

Nar. Dried millet, wẹsẹ.

Ch. Wẹsẹ.

Nar. Let Poling stop there.

EPISODE 16

Poling Fights Gemila

Nar. Gemila is powerful, eh, nalong ma zing.
Ziki-zing nalong-oh, Gemila is powerful.

Ch. Nalong ma zing, ziki-zing.
Gemila is powerful.

Nar. Dried millet, węsę.

The thing that makes a bad name for me here. Respond to the song. Respond so that my name goes to Geu. Don't respond so that when I sing it with my voice, it becomes bad. If my bad name remains in the mouths of these people, they will not again send for me. Do you hear? I didn't know here as of old. But the child has caused me to know here, and I will be coming here every Saturday. Wednesday. Do you hear? I didn't know here. So respond well to the song, what I can do I will do. When I'm going I go.

Do you hear?

So the song I am showing, they say, "Gemila is powerful." Eh, Poling is coming. But I fall again on this one. But Gemila is powerful and fights.
Poling is coming to catch Gemila.

Gemila is powerful, eh, nalong ma zing.
Poling is coming to catch Gemila.
Gemila is powerful, nalong ma zing.
Gemila is powerful.

Ch. Nalong ma zing ziki-zing nalong ma-oh.

Nar. Ah-oh, Boi has dropped Gemila.

Eh-eh, that's the song.

Sun-falling Boi has dropped Gemila.
Oh, dropping Gemila.
Dropping Gemila, oh.

Aud. My friend, whose song is that?

Nar. Is there no one here to sing Gemila?
Is there no one here to sing Gemila?
Zi, zi, zi, zi.

That's the song.

Eh, Boi dropped Gemila.

Q. They say there is no one to beat him.

Nar. There is no one to beat him and when he beats someone, he takes out his eyeballs.

Q. Oh.

Nar. Wọi's vehicle is really in the sky. They said, "Then fight and let us see."

Ah-oh, Boi has dropped Gemila.
Ah-oh, Boi has dropped Gemila.
He has dropped Gemila.
Eh, Gemila is powerful.
Boi has dropped Gemila.
Eh, Gemila is powerful.
Kpulung, kpulung, kpulung, kpulung, kpung, kpo, kpoko.

I have just plucked out your eyeballs, fall behind me.
He beats someone and takes out his eyeballs.

Q. Oh, my friend, but then it is spoiled. I want to know, that Gemila, does he have another Kpelle name?

Nar. His Kpelle name you will hear. And that is what angered Wọi in the fighting village. And he said he couldn't fight here. "Who is here who can fight the war with me? Let the people show their style for me to see."

Kulung, kulung, kulung, kulung, kpung, kpoko.

When I take out your eyeballs, just drop behind me.

Q. Oh, my friend.

Aud. Are those his fighting words?

Nar. Those are his fighting words.

Ee, maa-laa-kẹ-ma, oh.
Ah-oh, who drops Gemila.
Dropping Gemila.
Ee, there is none here to drop Gemila.
There is no one to drop Gemila, eh.
Ee, who can drop Gemila.
There is no one to drop Gemila, eh.
Ah-oh, who can drop Gemila.
A person to drop Gemila isn't here.
Ah-oh, who can drop Gemila.
Kpulung, kpulung, kpulung, kpulung, kpung, kpoko.

I take out your eyeballs. They said, "That is a fine matter."
They said, "The thing that Gemila is doing here is big."
Poling got up and said, "I will beat it in the morning."

Q. My friend, what thing and Poling smart like that?

Nar. Poling, you yourself know Poling. She is really fine.

Q. I know Poling. She is really fine.

Nar. Poling said, "I can beat Gemila." They went and reported to Wọi. Wọi said, "Well, what should I do? I am in the sky and I cannot come down. So what Gemila is doing to people spoiling their eyes, and you sit and watch. When he has spoiled all your eyes, I am not responsible." Poling said, they said to Poling's mate, "Then do it to Gemila in order for us to get out of the land." They will be able to it. You yourself, a woman doesn't give up on a person. You yourself, Poling is fine.
You know female Poling.
She said, "That is a fine matter." She said, "Well, I'm the one courting Poling. I'm the one courting Gemila."
Isn't that right? Mm.
She has agreed to it. Poling went, I tell you. They really dressed her. I tell you her neck was all beautifully designed.
I tell you, really. They dressed her, I tell you.
Poling came out and stepped outside, "Po."
Dried millet, wẹsẹ.

Ch. Wẹsẹ.

EPISODE 17

Poling Fights Gemila

Nar. Poling is fine, eh.
Dameyaa, Poling is fine, dameyaa.
Dameyaa, dameyaa, Poling is fine, eh.[39]
That is a fine song. Respond underneath the song well.
Eh, Maa-laa, bring me my voice-eh.
Eh, Maa-laa, bring my voice.
Ah-oh, look at Poling with the carved beads on her.
Poling is stalking, oh.

Q. Oh, my friend, what is Poling going to do?

Nar. She said, "I can beat Gemila in the morning."
And Gemila is lying in his house.

Q. Is Poling stalking outside?

---

39. Here the song of Episode Fifteen is repeated without explanation despite Kulung's assertion that songs are not to be repeated.

Nar. Poling is stalking outside. She says that Gemila can't come outside because of the way he breaks all of the town people's eyes. And when they say "Gemila-eye-breaking," that is the name of a grasshopper.

Q. Yes.

Nar. Don't you know that grasshopper?

Q. I know it.

Nar. Do you know its fingernails?

Q. Yes.

Nar. Eh, Maa-laa, bring my voice.

Q. Poling, you fine, clever thing.

Nar. She won't kill it fast, what can Poling do? Poling is stalking, she is stalking the town. Really, she has on beautiful pants. She has on carved beads. Her mate wears them. She says that she has carved beads. Hawk says to her, "That is a fine matter." She said, "Mm."
He said, "I am the one sitting behind you."
Eagle said, "I am the one sitting behind you."
He said, "Do you see my wife? Do you see the carved beads on her? Do you see the beautiful pants on her? Do you see the red head-scarf on her head?"
Gemila, the way he breaks a person's eyes, he is not there.
They said, "She will not do it." They said to her, "But don't jump on him, try to break his arm."
They all have gathered. They all have gathered in order, the person that took Gemila out of his house, when she comes they will crowd around her. Eagle and others were sitting. Poling and others were seated there.

Dried millet, wẹsẹ.

Ch. Wẹsẹ.

CHAPTER 3

Dried Millet Breaking

The detail of the pattern is movement,
As in the figure of the ten stairs.

T. S. Eliot
"Four Quartets"

The never-ending and eternal nature of wọi-mẹni-pele is but one facet of epic. Equally as important and related are the separate pieces of the Kpelle image that underlie that unity.

MOVEMENT

The Kpelle, first of all, delight in action. They notice, point to, and comment upon the quality of many kinds of movement. In the Wọi epic, Kulung dramatizes Spider playing the Slit-Drum, the blacksmith forging iron, the cowbird pumping the bellows for the blacksmith, Wọi's wife carving bowls, Wọi's house moving, and the men chopping an obstacle tree. The chorus echoes the visual-kinesthetic action with sounds: keng keree; keleng, keleng, zang, zang, keleng; zi, zi, zi; vẹ, vẹ; bongkai, kpolong, kpolong, fẹẹ-laa; zou, zou.

The episode of the banished wife carving bowls for a living shows this in some detail. Not content to simply portray the carving action with a "chop, chop," Kulung draws from an arsenal of onomatopoeic terms to imply carving of different qualities: bongkai "large inside," kpolong "thin walls," koro-koro "small adze strokes," mọnọ-mọnọ "shiny blackness," fẹẹ-laa "smooth." He luxuriates in a beautiful bowl. In contrast, when a woman, a most unwelcome client, appears, a single word depicts the carving: kpitili "thick, ugly." Such sensitivity is not surprising among a people who have at least six different words to describe the trembling motion of a dancer. Vowel colors and consonant sounds paint the sonic nuances for listeners, nuances they are accustomed to noticing in everyday life. The singer's gestures, as well, underscore visually the very lively soundscape. Each word of onomatopoeia engenders its own motion.

The movement in epic, however, does not give rise to the marked cutoffs that identify nonritual kinds of performances. The end of an episode is rather obscured. Though Kulung employs the formulaic ending cue "Dried millet, węsę" and the chorus responds "Węsę," he masks the segmentation. This he does by moving immediately into the next episode, by foreshadowing upcoming episodes, and by constantly introducing new characters and themes, many of whom are never explored or developed. Thus, the pieces and bits exist in epic, but with a difference.

THE PATH IMAGE

Kulung moves down the path of creating the epic in a circuitous fashion. He darts from one topic to another, from one focus to another, and never dwells in one spot very long. Consider the following excerpt:

Episode 2

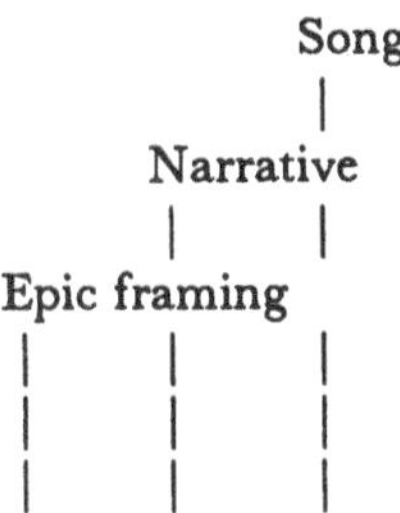

Nar. My fellow, answer man, answer man.

It's the diviner of the hole that they are calling. It was Wọi's wife who was pregnant, and they are calling diviner from the anteater's hole.

You, yourself, the head of an epic doesn't come out. You just keep bouncing.

They are going for divination. And the diviner of the anteater's hole is in the road. He comes to him and says to him, "Then here I am."

"Come and divine for me."

Ee, what does Maa-laa-kę-ma say?
Go, call the diviner of the anteater's hole to come.
Go, call the diviner of the anteater's hole to come.

In rapid succession the singer moves from exhorting the chorus, "My fellow, answer man, answer man," to narration, "It's the diviner of the hole that they are calling," to explanation to the audience about the structure of an epic, "You, yourself, the head of an epic does not come out," back to narration, "They are going for divination . . . "and then to the more reflective song, "Ee, what does Maa-laa-kę-ma say?" He first establishes the frame of epic, then narrates the story, only to go back to framing the epic before returning to narration and finally to the song, the most abstract expression form and innermost frame of the epic. Almost like a juggler, he never lets one aspect alone too long as he flits back and forth from one to another. The audience, who is singing the chorus and playing the instruments, provides a drone-like backdrop of song so that even when Kulung is not singing, music is ever present.

The frames of performance might better be thought of as circles, from the Kpelle point of view (see fig. 6). The first circle is the largest and most encompassing, containing all other circles. These circles agree with the indentation of text, the first circle corresponding with the text set in the left-most position. The fourth circle is an exception and is not indicated by indentation since it is embedded within the song. References to Poro in the song, however, are cued by a change in Kulung's voice timbre. He shifts to a distinctly nasal and muffled vocal quality. Kulung's signaling is not a personal idiosyncrasy, for I have noted this among other Kpelle singers performing other genres.

Figure 6. Circles of Epic Performance

1. Construction details (ordinary speech)
    2. Narration of story (heightened prose and poetic speech)
        3. Song within story (pourer and responding-underneath people) (song)
            4. Reference to Poro within song within story (song with nasal timbre)

A fundamental kind of movement in Kpelle life is walking. The Kpelle frequently describe performing as traveling down a path. Participants who move down the road together are said to have achieved some degree of synchrony. Conversely, when they move down different paths, their playing and singing has not properly meshed. "If people are responding underneath it badly, his voice goes on this path, his fellow's voice goes on that path" (Stone 1979:139-40).

The path is an apt metaphor, for it is fundamental to Kpelle life. Paths connect towns and link settlements to outlying farms. The paths wind through the trees and thick tropical undergrowth. They ascend hills and cross creeks. With villages as the nodes, paths become the connections between the nodes. But, as I discovered, paths should not be equated with lines and linearity, for in Kpelleland these paths are curved and crooked. Furthermore, the Kpelle do not measure paths in quantitative terms. They have difficulty estimating distance in units smaller than a day's walk. When asked how far a town is up ahead they often respond that it is just over the hill, whether it is a few or many miles ahead.[40]

40. This concept is part of the idea presented earlier of rhythmic patterns centering on a call-and-response conversation principle of organization.

Analogous to a path is the "groove" that the drummers in the African-derived Santeria cult in New York strive to create. They achieve the groove when the group's playing fits together properly and "the energy of the music becomes constant" (Friedman 1982:143).

The kinds of action executed by a character become vital in wọi-mẹni-pele. Action creates the epic in much the same way that action shows theme and character in Xhosa narrative tradition. According to Harold Scheub,

> Movement is vital to the tradition, action is all important, and character is revealed not by description but through action. Similarly, theme is revealed not by interpolations or preachments, but through action. (1970:144)

The Wọi epic action, which is first revealed in little parts, like the chopping of the bowl carver or the pumping of the iron-forging bellows, thrives at broader levels as well. The action is also unfolded in the series of confrontations that Wọi experiences as he moves his house. The fights with the Bẹlẹ-Tree, the Koing-Tree, and the pumpkin each last two episodes while the fight with the bat lasts but one episode.

Action is shown as well in the movement of the house itself as it proceeds ahead. Episodes Six and Eight are devoted to depicting that motion:

Zi, zi, zi, zi, zi . . . .
Q. What thing's sound is that again?
Nar. The house's traveling sound that is.
Q. Oh-koo. [expression of astonishment]
Nar. The house has risen into the distant sky. The house is going.
Q. Wọi's house?
Nar. Wọi's house.
Q. Were you there?
N. Very close, really.
All the things were responding. I tell you the gboto frogs in the swamp were responding, "Wọi, wọi." Do you know gboto's voice? There's the house they are announcing. Isn't it so?

All this action and confrontation does not lead, however, to a definitive climax. Each small crisis is resolved and the house moves on to the next challenge. The lack of linear progression between episodes in the Wọi and in some other African epics is very reminiscent of the situation that Alton L. Becker describes for Javanese shadow theater (wayang kulit). A wayang plot is built on coincidence and may begin at any point in the story temporally. Becker comments that "to focus on, for instance, causal sequences and character development is to miss the area of relevant variation in wayang theater and to miss the subtlety and depth of a good wayang" (1979:219). Robert Plant Armstrong's textual analysis of the musical-drama *The Palm Wine Drinkard* from

Nigeria identifies the episodes as "sequential" rather than "consequential" in what he terms "intensive continuity." He notes that "continuity can be seen as a function of the density of multiple, discrete parts" (1971:168).

PIECING AND PLACING

The Kpelle delight in segmenting performance into discrete little units that are also part of a larger fabric. In this they are not so unlike the Shona with their "kaleidophonic" music (Berliner 1978:111). Much like a quilter, the Kpelle take tiny pieces and arrange and rearrange them in the course of creating the epic. The chorus is a supporting singer's part pieced into the space between the end of the choral pattern and the beginning of the next repetition. Like a dovetail, the two create the impression of one single pattern, so neatly do they join (see fig. 7). The epic singer moves from instructing the chorus in this technique, to singing the signature song for the episode, to narrating, each piece of a different sort but fit seamlessly together into a smooth and continuous exposition.

Figure 7. Chorus/Song Catcher Composite, Episode 3

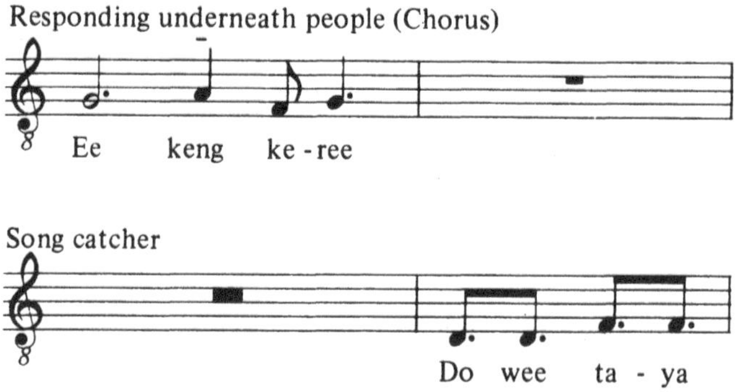

Responding underneath people (Chorus)

Ee keng ke - ree

Song catcher

Do wee ta - ya

Beginnings in the epic, like in other music, are often extended. The singer builds his groups and tunes them in to one another, slowly refining their sounds by prodding and demonstrating. Endings, however, appear to be more abrupt. The epic episode ends with the simple spoken phrase, "Dried millet, wẹsẹ." This is not unlike the case Charles Keil describes for the Tiv of Nigeria: "Songs begin with a purposeful burst but end only by accident or necessity, or so it seems" (1979:18). Among the Diola-Fogny, however, the ending must be done with some skill: "The singer . . . looks for the road by which he is to kill so that everyone in the ensemble will hear the song and remember it" (Sapir 1969:178).

Breaking up of parts is not unique to the epic. Indeed, for the Kpelle the highest form of performance is hocketing, as seen in bush-clearing songs. Here each performer sings from one to a maximum of three notes which are interlocked with the note or notes of the other performers and hence of the group, and all of the notes performed together form a composite melody. Requiring intense synchronization of timing, this performance is highly admired. Nor does it seem that this love of small parts is restricted to music making. Susan Vogel has noted for the Baule of Ivory Coast that a cardinal feature of the visual art is its "segmented quality" (Thompson 1974).

In each of the epic's episodes, the choral ostinato hints at and, in a sense, is a capsule summary of the episode. Subsequent imagery and action simply unfold what was presented in miniature and encapsulated in the ostinato. The development thus becomes that of expansion rather than linear movement. And yet this choral part is often very brief, interlocking ever so deftly with the supporting soloist part, which is also short. In the case of the jealous wife (Episode Five), each of these parts consists only of several syllables.

S.S.	Ee-oo, bowl, mother, mother.
Ch.	Bowl, mother.
Nar.	Only the bowl owner knows its price.

Here, according to Kpelle people who know this epic, the bowl, symbol of the woman's physical lust and jealousy and carved to satisfy her desires, is placed next to the term "mother" (lee). A more dichotomous contrast is difficult to find. Then the last line explains a bit more of the plight. It implies that the shame of having to get sex through charging rests with the woman. The knowledge of the pain is known to her alone.

The bowl represents both means of livelihood and disgrace. The terms used to describe the carving of the bowl can also be understood to apply to a woman's vagina. Thus, on one level the narrator is describing a bowl, but on another level he is simultaneously giving us an image of the vagina, all done through symbolic representation. The bowl and the vagina are bound together in imagery. The situation expands further when after the first act of bowl carving the narrator sings, "Sun-falling, Maa-laa, what do you say?" addressing his tutelary spirit and adding yet another participant from the supernatural to enhance the images as sounded.

We know that the rich bowl-carving sounds are no accident when a female client happens along and the sounds of carving change for her. A single sound, "kpitili," is used a few times, indicating something thick and ugly. The humorous contrast of the two responses to clients heightens the scene already drawn.

It appears, then, that the shifting from narration to abstract song and from commentary to dialogue presents different perspectives of the same theme. What must be understood is the base idea. Then one can see why the narrator has allowed two apparently dissimilar things to coincide. In seeing things in a new constellation, the audience recognizes a fresh meaning. The episode of the jealous wife is not simply an incident of entertainment. Sounds of carving a beautiful bowl are set next to sounds of carving an ugly bowl to show a theme of some prominence in Kpelle folklore. The theme of jealous co-wives recalls an area of great concern and attention in everyday Kpelle life. And, as a vital part of the summary of Kpelle life, this episode qualifies for being of the Wọi epic.

One more example will show the deliberateness of construction details. In Episode Two, which concerns the divination before Wọi's wife gives birth to all living things, the ostinato refrain of the the chorus is "Ziang-kpono." Ziang is a kind of tree composed of very dense wood. Kpono is body. This phrase indicates the weight and importance of matters to occur in this episode. Both the divination and the creation of living things are compared to such density.

THE PAST IN THE PRESENT

The pieces that build performance are drawn from different time dimensions as well as different space dimensions. Kulung is fond of singing phrases such as "Oh, Maa-laa, bring my voice," and "Maa-laa doesn't fool around." These address no one physically present at the event and they do not comment on any characters that are part of the Wọi epic. Rather, Kulung is here appealing to a tutelary spirit, a supernatural being normally living in a distinctly different space, who assists his performance. Like many other Kpelle artists, Kulung is in a demanding, and often difficult, relationship, filled with potential treachery. Though Kulung, with this special aid, became a competent musician, he is often threatened by insanity or death if the cunning female tutelary's demands cannot be met.

Although Kulung, like many other performers, is circumspect about these private relationships, among the Kpelle the spirit reveals itself most frequently in the sphere of dreaming, nyii-pere (sleep road), and manifests itself in performance events at specific times (Stone 1982:85). A Kpelle tutelary may also be the spirit of a deceased great performer who comes back to lend greatness to music making. The most desirable tutelary spirit among the neighboring Gola of Liberia is one which is associated with an ancestor and comes from a group of neme that other kinsmen share (d'Azevedo 1973:295).

There are other surrogate participants besides the tutelary spirit who may participate in the event. These may be recognized by only a select part of the audience. Some, as *predecessors,* are beings who share neither time nor space. They live in the land of the ancestors. Others, like Kulung's tutelary, Maa-laa-kẹ-ma, are *contemporaries,* beings who share time but not space. In both cases they are transformed in the event into *consociates*, individuals who briefly share both time and space during the performance (Stone 1982:84). In the epic, Maa-laa-kẹ-ma, a contemporary tutelary spirit, becomes a consociate for a short and temporary period. In other events, where deceased performers enliven the performance, the past also becomes part of the present in a very active way.

For the Kpelle, then, beneath the outer layer of continuity lies a mosaic of movements and pieces. The outer crust, in which the "head doesn't come out," conceals the core that is vital and segmented. "We cut it short, short." The continuity is thus a pulsing, living kind of performance, not a static piece of sound sculpture.

CHAPTER 4

Exchanges That Keep the Epic Going

The length of the epic, performed with all the elaboration of chorus, questioner, and dramatic gestures, depends upon the mutual audience-performer feeling. Any episode, or, for that matter, the entire evening's performance, hangs on the excitement that develops or doesn't develop, as the case may be. The text that exists prior to any rendition is a series of motifs or patterns waiting to be placed in what will be a unique arrangement, albeit with some recognizable elements. Wọi epic is not by any means a verbatim text awaiting recitation.

Little gifts given at intervals index the audience's feeling. These tokens, cigarettes, cane juice, palm wine, or coins, undergirded by a speech of carefully shaped oratory, indicate approval. Without the continuing of such audience sentiment, the teller regretfully terminates the event at an early point. Thus, it is vital to attend to the timing aspect of these rewards, the nature of these tokens of appreciation, and their significance to the dynamics of the event. The importance of continued gifts and the interval of timing has been studied by the noted French sociologist Pierre Bordieu in his work among the Kabyle of Algeria. He speaks of the "infinite multiplication of the infinitely small, in the form, for example, of the 'little present' said to 'keep friendship going'" (1977:7). This timing has been noted in other epic performance as well. Albert Lord, the noted Serbo-Croatian epic scholar, says,

> It is more likely that, instead of having this ideal occasion the singer will realize shortly after beginning that his audience is not receptive, and hence he will shorten his song so that it may be finished within the limit of time for which he feels the audience may be counted upon. Or, if he misjudges, he may simply never finish the song. (1960:16-17)

The giving of gifts also brings complications. Near the end of Episode Seven, some beer is given to the performers. As it is presented Kulung asks, "Am I doing it?" and someone from the audience replies, "You are doing it well." The questioner chimes in, "You are trying." Kulung responds, "Is that right? I told you four days," to recall one performance where he claims to have continued for four days. Someone in the audience queries, "What were you doing with it?" Kulung comes back, "We were doing it. Man, give me my beer." An audience member replies, "Yours is there." Kulung complains to the other performers, "You have drunk yours and you say this? Stop, a person doesn't do things like that." The audience, nevertheless, is anxious to hear more of the story, and the questioner, unconcerned about the sharing of the beer among chorus and singer, continues, "This bow that is talking with its owner, I want to hear its song." Kulung, not to be deprived of his beer, picks up a bottle and starts to drink from it, "Isn't this mine?" The questioner responds, "You should just be concerned to sing songs. Yours is inside it," meaning that Kulung's greater reward will come later with a fine performance. Kulung, finally persuaded, then says, "Leave mine in the bottle," and the performance continues.

Performers of all kinds in Kpelleland relish relating stories of when they excelled in performance and their client was so moved that he or she abandoned customary common sense to offer extravagant gifts: a gown, or a prized tobacco box. The music had, in fact, transformed the client to interpret the situation differently than he or she would have done in everyday life. When such an elaborate gift was given, the audience was sometimes infected and likewise, without having intended to do so, gave ever more elegant tokens. But such, say the Kpelle, can be the power of music.[41]

Turn taking in everyday Kpelle talk means frequent change of speakers. In the epic text itself are embedded a number of these typical exchanges of rapid-fire turn taking. From Episode Four, where the tuu-tuu bird, also known as Kelema-ninga, pumps the bellows, the narrator says,

> Wọi said, "It is a good matter."
> Then Kelema-ninga said, "Mm."
> He said, "You."
> He said, "Mm."
> He said, "You."
> He said, "Mm."
> He said, "It's you who is not forging the iron so I am not able to go and fight." He said, "You blowing the bellows."
> He said, "Mm."
> He said, "Then you have sleeping sickness. Let me take the cutlass iron."

This interchange between performer and audience involves an element of power and the manipulation of that power over time. Kulung, while apparently quite powerful to authorize certain people to fill roles that may offer more or less latitude for turn taking, is monitored by audience approval. Kenneth Gourlay, British ethnomusicologist, describes how turn taking demonstrates power

41. For a detailed description of transformations that may occur in a performance, see Kapferer's study of Sri Lankan exorcism rituals (1979).

among the Karimojong of northeastern Uganda. A dozen or so people gather for beer parties and sing ox-songs. Each song, consisting of a solo-and-chorus structure, has a different individual as soloist. The upcoming potential soloist—not the then-currently-performing soloist—determines when the song before his will terminate. When the complete chorus is sung, the new leader begins his song at once. Gourlay notes that on one occasion two young men were so carried away with their singing that they failed to hear the terminating cue and were severely reprimanded by the oldest woman present. The turn-taking mechanism helps to avoid overly eager soloists; "should anyone rush in to end a performance after three or four solo-chorus sequences without the support of the group, he faces not merely social disapproval for bad manners, but the social prospect of having his song 'stopped' after only two!" (Gourlay 1972:241-42).

The very structuring of Kpelle epic chorus around the perpetual exchange of small bits of sound builds momentum and energy that fuel the spoken narration. The Kpelle are very aware of energy levels in performance and admire performance that is highly energized. Music creates energy that must underlie performance (see Schieffelin 1985:714).

EXCHANGES AND TRANSFORMATION

The Wọi epic, through the exchanges, transforms listeners into a group with certain shared loyalties by reminding them of salient and crucial elements in their heritage. They identify with Wọi, a hero who overcomes obstacles through supernatural power, allies, and cunning. He, more than any other character of the aesthetic imagination, represents for the Kpelle a group hero and symbol. And through this identification with Wọi, the Kpelle also accomplish a transformation from identifying simply with their local group or community to sharing the intricate beauty and hilarity of a larger commonality.

The Kpelle also maintain that in performance the experience of everyday life will be transformed and altered. Performance becomes a crucial act in transforming sadness or happiness in everyday life into tranquility. A somewhat similar case of transformation is noted by anthropologist Peter Rigby among the Gogo of Tanzania; in Gogo rituals of purification a transformation is accomplished whereby time is "re-reversed" to bring about a good state of affairs. Music and role reversal work together to accomplish this. Women, rather than men, sing lewd songs and dance away the contamination. Thus, symbolic reversal in a world reversed achieves transformation to the normal good state (Rigby 1968:159, 172).

The Wọi epic offers comic situations, pathetic dilemmas, and rich reminders of heritage. One ritual specialist related to me a myth of the origin of music.

> What I know about song, it comes from sadness. Our old people, their old people, went to Spider for divination. If it is so, you have a child, it dies, what

> can make you forget? Your child, you the father, if you die, what can make your child forget? And so Spider spoke and said, "That's good." Sadness brings laughter. Even if your heart hurts, you must laugh. Even if you cry and you do everything, you must perform [music]. . . . If your heart hurts, you can't sit quietly again. Before you sit quietly, you must sing so your heart forgets in your stomach.
>
> . . . When they are performing fiya-le [cry uttered upon the birth of a child] event, all the women will perform, all the men will perform. Then, today you are creating child performance. You don't know its stomach [intention]. If it will go back, you don't know. If it will thrive, you don't know. That is the second source of performance. (Stone 1975:1-2)

Victor Turner (1967:106) has also considered transformations in events, pointing to the state of communitas, also labeled as transition by Arnold van Gennep and occurring in rites of passage between phases of separation and incorporation (van Gennep 1960). In communitas the participants achieve a special communion among themselves, a catharsis brought about by separation from their old status and the groups they formerly associated with as well as by their distance from their new group, into which they are not yet incorporated. In musical events, then, such transformations are often tied to and integrally linked with the music sound production. While Rodney Needham, the British social anthropologist, has made a rather sweeping link between percussion instruments being played and transition from one status to another such as occurs in rites of passage (1967:606-14), more ethnographic data are required. Whatever the legitimacy of Needham's statement, his essay suggests that in Africa, and elsewhere, certain instruments appear crucial to marking time passage in the social life of an individual. An ethnomusicologist might argue that in Africa the presence of percussion is so pervasive that it is essential to the creation of music for any purpose on any occasion. If an instrument is not what might be classified as percussive by ethnomusicologists, it is nevertheless played in a percussive manner by the performer. Whatever the accompanying instruments for the Kpelle, performance, in which music is a critical element, transforms people who are emotionally charged with happiness or sadness and helps them become calm again.

TRANSACTION IN MUSICAL TIME

The idea of exchange is very prominent as we begin to understand African music from the point of view of Africans themselves. The way the Wọi epic divides every choral motif into a call-response phrase beautifully illustrates the principle. In Episode One, the chorus completes its phrase before the song catcher begins (see fig. 8). In another episode, however, the choral motif is very short and persists in ostinato fashion while the supporting singer sings (see fig. 9).

Figure 8. Choral Motif Exchange, Episode 1

Responding underneath people (Chorus) I

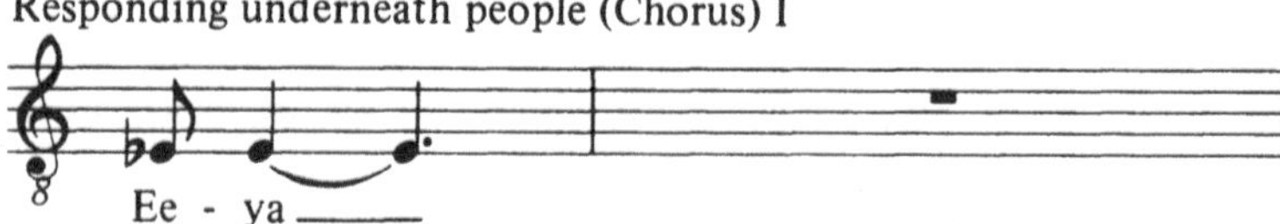

Responding underneath people (Chorus) II

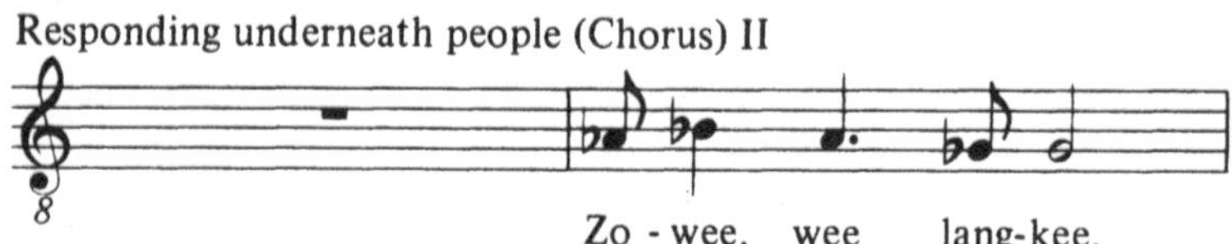

Figure 9. Choral Motif Exchange, Episode 4

Responding underneath people (Chorus) I

Vee mm, vee mm, vee mm,

Responding underneath people (Chorus) II

Gerhard Kubik points out that two players of Mangwilo xylophone in southeast Africa sit opposite one another and both share in playing the same instrument. They are referred to as Opachera (the starting one) and Wakulela (the responding one) (1965:36). Similarly, Paul Berliner shows that even with a solo instrument like the plucked idiophonic mbira of Zimbabwe, the Shona people designate the first part as "kushaura (to lead the piece, to take the solo part)" and the second part as the "kutsihira (to exchange parts of a song; to interweave a second interlocking mbira part)" (1978:73). The Shona people praise the mbira for complexity, saying that "it sounds like many instruments being played at once" (1978:23).

If exchange or transaction is primary in conceiving of rhythm, then the search for a unifying beat by which all performers measure and calculate their performance becomes less important and less likely to provide an answer to how Africans organize time. Rather, the answer may be closer to what Kubik identifies as the "interlocking" style, where each Mangwilo xylophone player feels his own pulse and the two mesh when heard as one into yet another unity (1965:39). The importance of the two parts may be illustrated in the difficulty a dondon (hourglass drum) player experiences playing one part at a time, even though the beats of each part cross when the two parts combine in performance. The drummer complains that he cannot "hear" his part without the second drum playing (Chernoff 1979:53).

The idea that drums and other instruments converse in a kind of exchange is an oft-expressed idea of African musicians (Chernoff 1979:53). What has been, in the past, used as a formal characteristic of vocal music applies equally as well for other media. Thus, rather than conceive of African music as focusing on one beat to which all other parts fit, we need to explore the possibility that the key rests within the dynamic tension between two parts, which converse through time. John Blacking supports the exchange principle by showing that musicians use it, not out of necessity but for aesthetic quality:

> Thus, performances by combinations of two or three players of rhythms that can, in fact, be played by one are not musical gimmicks: they express concepts of individuality in community, and of social, temporal, and spatial balance, which are found in other features of Venda culture and other types of Venda music. (1973:30)

BACKGROUND TO TRANSACTION

Transaction, a key concept in African music making, has developed from a number of related ideas. Though some researchers assumed an equal pulse base (Merriam 1977), other ethnomusicologists sensed that the timing had some not-so-equal and not-so-regular patterns as measured in Western terms. Thus some asserted that African music exhibits an "off-beat" characteristic (Locke 1978:349; Chernoff 1979:47-48), also called "syncopation."

Off-beat phrasing and syncopation imply that a steady, equally spaced beat underlies the performance. Another part is conceived in *relation* to that beat and as the two parts are heard together, the second is playing off the beat. The first part, rather than the second, is considered to be on the beat. The distinction is important because a question can be raised as to whether, in fact, the two parts might be more adequately analyzed as moving in rhythms where each maintains its own *beat*, albeit beats that do not coincide.

Rose Brandel, among others, has argued that what might be identified as syncopation or off-beat phrasing is better described as hemiola. Following the lead of her mentor Curt Sachs she notes, "The African hemiola style is based on this play of two and three, which is much like the Middle Eastern additive style of rhythm with its far greater diversity of durational contrast" (1961:15). Pulses are grouped together in units of two or three and they can exhibit the 2:3 ratio horizontally over time or vertically between parts. All of this makes possible unequally spaced beats without implying that the asymmetrical beats derive from a central beat.[42] John Blacking comments on the flexibility of interpretation that this makes possible when he refers to a 6/8 pattern:

42. For more details on this argument see Stone 1985.

> [W]hen it is played in Europe it is always conceived as the product of a single agent—with a very few possible exceptions. . . . In the African context the rhythm expresses the perfect cooperation of two performers who nevertheless preserve their individuality by maintaining different main beats. (1969:18)

Arthur M. Jones coined the term "cross rhythm," which describes a phenomenon similar to, but somewhat different from, hemiola (1934). Of cross rhythm he said,

> The melody being additive, and the claps being divisive, when put together they result in a combination of rhythms whose inherent stresses are *crossed.* This is of the very essence of African music: this is what the African is after. He wants to enjoy a conflict of rhythm. (1959:21-22)

In figure 10, the so-called time line, otherwise known as the "structural core" (Kubik 1983:38), "timekeeper" (Nketia 1958:21), or "standard pattern" (King 1960), shows the horizontal play of two against three in one of its possible common notational forms. The time line in this form occurs in the first bottle pattern of Episode One (see fig. 10) and is well known among the Kpelle.

Figure 10. Time Line.[43]

```
12/8   x • x • x x • x • x x •
       2+  2+  3+    2+  3
```

INNER TIME

Time which passes by the movement on a clock or by the beating of a drum is but one dimension of what Alfred Schutz, a philosopher-sociologist in the area of phenomenology, calls outer time (1971). By his definition nearly everything ethnomusicologists study under the heading of rhythm would fit into this category. The patterns of the struck bottles in the Wọi epic would be rhythms in outer time.

Schutz points out that in his view there is more to time. The heart and soul of music, Schutz contends, is the inner time dimension which is also present (Skarda 1979:77). While such coordination is a prerequisite, the richness of music arises from the inner time, and Schutz says,

> The flux of tones unrolling in inner time is an arrangement meaningful to both the composer and the beholder, because and in so far as it evokes in the stream of consciousness participating in it an interplay of recollections, retentions,

43. x = struck; • = rest or sustained.

> protentions, and anticipations which interrelate the successive elements. (1971:170)

Such time, by virtue of being nonquantitative, at least in Schutz's reflection about Western music, is not measured by clocks or metronomes and yet it is coordinated to this outer time as the multiple temporal streams move together. This inner time might also be known as the "high" people report feeling or the "flow" they experience once outer time is under full control. Though very little literature in African music documents the fascinating dimension of inner time, several ethnomusicologists provide ethnographic examples of what appears to be inner time.

Alan Boyd, an ethnomusicologist working in the Muslim community of Lamu, Kenya, describes visible interplay of inner and outer time in the maulidi events, musical performances that include recitations from the Quran interspersed with hymns. Participants move toward inner time by coordinating a unison swaying motion. He says,

> The rhythms accompanying the hymn are steady at first, but are increased in intensity as the chorus is sung by everyone. As each verse is begun by an individual, the drummers relax the pulse, but as soon as the group joins in they increase the volume, the tempo and the intensity of the beat. During the repetitions, the tempo becomes steadily more forceful, emphasizing the motions of the dancers. (1977:8)

While such activity facilitates meditation and the experiencing of inner time vividly, certain circumstances may counteract transformation in the audience's awareness. Boyd gives an instance when people had difficulty forgetting about outer time. An inexperienced frame-drum player was tolerated for some time by the audience. But as group coordination became more crucial toward the end of the hymn, an older drummer moved in and replaced him and, as Boyd reports, there was an "audible communal sigh" (1977:9).

Paul Berliner, in his study of mbira performance among the Shona of Zimbabwe, vividly describes aspects of what I have here termed inner time though he does not label it as such. He sketches a scene one morning at sunrise following an all-night ceremony for ancestral spirits; the people were exhausted from the effort spent and lack of sleep during the performance. Hakurotwo Mude, a mbira player, looked in the distance and quietly played his instrument, oblivious to his young son, who put a hand on his father's shoulder.

> As Mude played the mbira his eyes became clouded. Tears welled up and fell silently down his cheeks. It was some time before anyone noticed what was happening. Finally Mude's father-in-law walked over and knelt before him. Careful not to interfere with the playing of the mbira, the old man pulled a handkerchief out of his pocket and blotted up the tears on Mude's cheeks. Tears flowed so steadily that the old man saw it was to no avail. He stood up and silently motioned to all the other villagers seated around to follow him into

> the large kitchen where the bira had previously been held. So as not to embarrass Mude, we left him to his music and his tears. (1978:132)

The evidence seems to indicate that Mude was focusing his awareness in inner time, where, through music, his experience moved him to tears. We are inferring such a conclusion, of course, for we cannot, as is the case in all social research, examine his mind directly. Mude was obviously not concentrating on the timing of his music or on the physical act of creating it, for that seemed almost automatic. This example brings to the fore very clearly the fact that music experience in inner time involves the human emotions in a central way. A quantitative analysis can hardly give us a satisfactory explanation or a complete explanation of what is happening in this kind of flow. We must grope with qualitative language to roughly, at least, communicate this very special quality of human experience.

Events are often structured temporally to facilitate the movement of participants from outer to inner time, sometimes over an extended period. James T. Brink, anthropologist, analyzes the kotè-tlon, a young people's dramatic musical event of the Bamana people of north-central Mali, and the timing of the overall evening's event. Each segment involves a slow to fast progression. The slow portion puts things in order and "enables the actors to assume the role of 'stupid' and to draw attention to the 'stranger' status of these stupid characters" (Brink 1981:28). The fast portion is the "laughing place," where the most critical and satirical material is placed. It is the fast tempo portions where the audience is moved to laughter and to move in inner time. During the slow tempo the basis for the experience is established and ordered, focusing on outer time.

Inner time is not, it should be mentioned, necessarily a mass group experience. That is, though many aspects of context may serve to induce an inner time experience, individuals, based on their interpretation of the situation, may or may not experience inner time. Furthermore, an individual may focus on inner time and then suddenly refocus on outer time as, perhaps, a tempo falters. Such changes can be very quick and thus any analysis must recognize the elasticity and flexibility of the human participant. As Paul Berliner emphasizes, the mbira player of Zimbabwe dwells on a wide range of subjects stimulated by the musical event. As Hakurotwo Mude told him: "When I play the mbira in Highfields [Salisbury], I can see places as far as my home in Mondoro or farther, and in my mind I am just [transported] there" (Berliner 1978:131).

As the audience of the Wọi epic gradually empathizes with the characters, laughs, and is astonished, they accomplish their transformation in a scene that is different from everyday life. Life is exaggerated, comic to the extreme, and overdrawn. As the audience enters the world of Wọi, they are experiencing inner time to the extent that they shift not only from attention to the mundane problems of life but also from the mechanics of the epic as it builds to deeper meanings and expressivity. The scenes that the singer builds are rearranged and special life. As one Kpelle commented while watching the videotape of the Wọi epic, "Things are different there, they will be there."

Though inner time has, up to this point, been treated in a monolithic fashion, certainly we would expect, with more research, to find it even more delineated. For example, we may describe that part of inner time which is a deeper experience than the ordinary inner time. When a person enters an inner time state he or she may be removed from ordinary outer time awareness. In such a state, body processes may be radically altered. In many African musical events, achieving an altered state is desirable for a number of the participants. Visible manifestations of this state may include very altered dance patterns, convulsive limb movements, and change in eye focus. In some situations, the individual is believed to be possessed by a deity who governs and orders his or her movements. Such experiences are considered peak moments for individuals in events influenced by cultural expectations and audience support.

While this study does not intend to provide a detailed discussion of altered states of consciousness, their connection to music and inner time needs to be established. A number of researchers point to the importance of drumming in inducing such states. In his recent study carried out in New World populations of African descendants, Robert Friedman provides information about events where altered states are important in Santeria, a religious practice deriving from Yoruba religion. In the events leading to an altered state of consciousness, the drums are believed to be surrogate humans and "talk" by reproducing phonemic pitch of the secret Lucumi dialect of Yoruba. As Friedman quotes one drummer,

> It's all three drums which make up the words. . . . That's six hands . . . whoever tries to put something different in there is a liar . . . you can't invent there. The conversations have to be there because the batá talk . . . that is the communication that is going on between the drums and the orisha [deity]. (1982:143)

Friedman goes on to describe the indications that an individual is entering an altered state and becoming possessed.

> The individual may appear to be completely involved in the dance activity to the extent that his movement becomes highly stylized, more accelerated and distinct from his preceding patterns of movement . . . the mounting process . . . is marked by the individual either falling to the floor in salutation or shouting a phrase in Lucumi. (1982:191)

Paul Berliner also looks at possession in the bira, the event for ancestral spirits that is often convened for healing. Here an ensemble of mbira dzavadzimu performs.

> As the music becomes intense and more participants enter into the performance, the suspense mounts. No one knows just when the possession of the

> medium (or mediums) will occur, or, at times, whom the spirits will possess. The spirits sometimes choose unsuspecting participants as their hosts. (Berliner 1978:190)

Berliner emphasizes that a musician possessed cannot simultaneously focus on performing properly. He describes a ceremony where a possessed participant began playing the hosho (rattle) violently. He overpowered the mbira and everyone was carried away by the spirit's behavior. The musicians later complained of his poor performance. He could not follow the mbira's rhythm or maintain a steady beat. Even though he was possessed his behavior was not entirely excused (1978:195-96). Thus we see that simply experiencing the recollections and protentions of music and entering an altered state of consciousness are quite different degrees of inner time. The deeper the altered state becomes, the less easily the individual can hold outer time even in his peripheral awareness. The paradox of the musical experience appears that the more deeply one experiences inner time, the greater the danger of losing awareness of the outer time and coordination necessary to continue the event.

The Wọi epic is created not to dwell on the coordination of the parts or of the chorus with the narrator or of the questioner with the narrator. That is only the beginning; the goal is, in fact, to move the audience to a deeper experience. As the audience laughs at the tuu-tuu bird falling asleep at his job when trying to pump the bellows, as they admire the bowl being carved chip by chip by the jealous woman, and as they sense danger as a monster blocks the path of Wọi's house, they can experience a sense of inner time. They approach that inner time through working together first in rhythmic coordination, and then, when they are able to continue that coordination on a kind of automatic pilot, they can shift to noticing inner time. Their experience in inner time will be that which they will recall and cherish if the performance moves them and affects them emotionally. It will be the kind of event that people will remember some six years later, as people did Kulung's memorable performance.

Kulung, epic performer from Central Kpelle area

Kulung

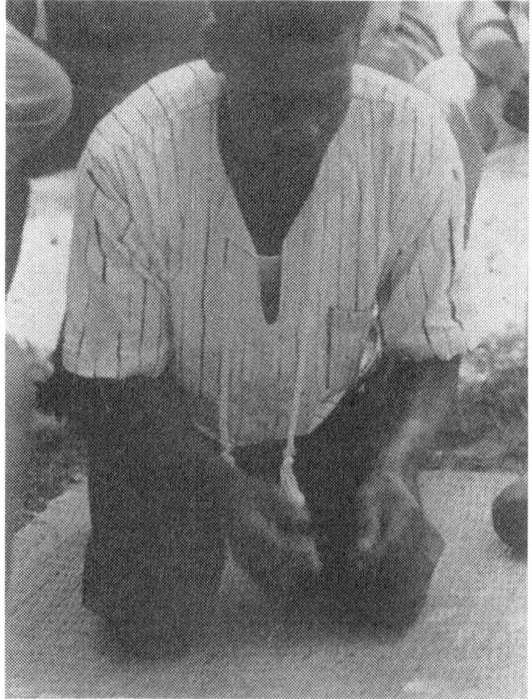

Kulung imitates Spider playing the slit drum

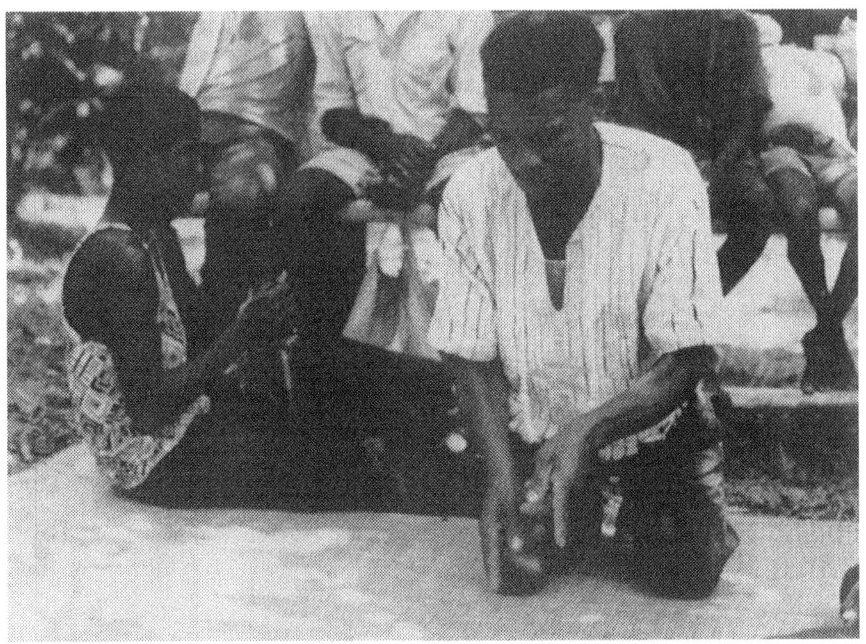

Bottle player provides rhythmic background

Sign in Monrovia uses "time" in a political message

A man in the Totota market with his alarm clock

Kulung depicts Spider eating a mound of rice

A path that has become a part-time motor road

CHAPTER 5

The Textured Moment in Epic

> The moment is the bed of the river of my thought. The pulsations of the moments have the pulsations of thought; the breath of thought glides into the blow-pipe of the moment. (Ouologuem 1971:165-66)

For the Kpelle of Liberia, wọi-mẹni-pele constitutes a place and time of action that is imbued with a certain separation from the ordinary ebb and flow of everyday life.[44] Participants comment, "ŋa lọi bệlei su (I'm entering the inside of the performance)" to show that things happening within an event of music, dance, and instrument playing are bounded from the rest of the world. Participants emphasize that even if there are disagreements prior to an event they need not and should not be brought into the event. They often begin an event with the words "Zu e nẹẹ (Let the inside be sweet)." What happens during epic performance is inside and the rest is outside.

The inside/outside distinction is also emphasized among the neighboring Kuranko of Sierra Leone in balancing the social order (Jackson 1977a:31),[45] among the Yoruba of Nigeria to distinguish eyes gods use to see the heavens and those they use to see men and women (Thompson 1983:9), and among the Tiv, also from Nigeria, to distinguish one's immediate surrounding from that with which one is not so familiar (Abraham 1940:27). The Kpelle are not unique in their emphasis on these dimensions in the performance of epic.

The use of the concept "moment" implies time that is not perceived to be moving forward linearly. From the Kpelle point of view this moment can expand much as a bubble which is gradually blown full of more and more air (Stone 1982:72). Furthermore, there are smaller moments within the large mo-

44. For more discussion of Kpelle music events, see Stone 1982.

45. The fact that Jackson labels the aspect of "inner" and "outer" as spatial should not negate their utility, for as we proceed we shall see how intertwined these notions of human experience—space and time—are in all world cultures.

ment of epic much like smaller bubbles that may be contained within the bubble one is blowing from soapy water.

The Wọi epic singer moves subtly and carefully to the inside of the performance. He does so by building the boundary that separates wọi-mẹni-pele in stages. When he has the chorus and instrumentalists interweaving their patterns in endless repetition, he has a beginning to the boundary. When the questioner asks his first question, "Whose voice is that?" the singer has his cue to begin building the narrative portion. Now there is not only epic being performed, but a distinctive story to be spun. The boundary adds up much like a crowd filling a Kpelle courtroom. First, people sit on the outer edges in front, on the sides, and at the back. Only with the border outlined do people begin to fill the middle, whether the room contains benches in straight rows or not. Once the narrator is moving within a particular part of the story he begins his embellishment and weaving that will distinguish him as an individual singer.

Within the Expandable Moment

At a variety of structural levels, moments envelop action with variable propensity to expand outward but not linearly. Such an approach to temporality recalls Georges Gurvitch's definition of time as a "continuity of heterogeneous moments" (1964:18).

Moments are built at a number of levels of specificity. On the most general level, an entire performance can be viewed as a moment qualitatively different from other moments within the flow of life. The Kpelle visually and kinesthetically circumscribe and bound the spatial dimensions of the place where this moment is experienced. As they enter a town to perform, musicians often process in a counterclockwise direction around the outer perimeter of the village, employing sound as a delineator and audio marker. As the spatial area is delineated, pệle, or the event, is freed of malevolent spirits and set apart from everyday life in the village.

On a more specific level, some moments exist coterminously with songs. Through creative improvisation, song (wule) is inflated to huge proportions. As one Kpelle performer explained, the longer one sings a song the more one builds it. On the conclusion of that song, however, a moment of very different sort may be closely juxtaposed. The expansion possibilities at all times are contingent upon many elements like audience response and performer synchronization.

On an even more specific level, within a song, observable moments can be delineated from other moments. Such is the case when the event clicks in synchronous precision and a solo dancer emerges in the dance arena to display her skill in artistic motion. Before the beginning of the dance proper she visibly defines the outer perimeter of her dancing stage as she regally moves counterclockwise to circumscribe the area and, concomitantly, the moment (Stone 1982:100-101).

Francis Bebey characterizes Gilbert Rouget's recording of Babinga Pygmy dance as constructed of a series of relatively short movements with interruptions (1975:128-30). In Hausa praise performance, the singer figuratively "blows up" a patron as a blacksmith pumps bellows, and thus the very audience member expands with the euphoria that the barrage of praises produces (Gidley 1975:98). Moments become, as Gurvitch notes of time, "convergent and divergent movements which persist in discontinuous succession" (1964:18).

Key moments within the Wọi epic use the ubiquitous Kpelle love for onomatopoeia. "Squirrel-Monkey has come out kili, kili, kili, kili." Contrast that with Ɣele-lawọ moving to battle, "va, va, va, va." Or, "Wọi's wife was pregnant *kpung-kung* (very pregnant)."

But these moments also build on proverbs and extracts. These nuggets embody so much, lead to so many associations, and move the audience to new heights by their particular positioning. Kulung opens the first episode with the assertion that he was with Wọi as he prepared to go to war. Kulung describes the people around Wọi as a "sitting-on-the-neck crowd." Sitting-on-the-neck refers to a mother with so many children that they hover around perched on her neck. To the Kpelle this is a very graphic and funny image.

In Episode Two Kulung uses two proverbs to inspire the instrumentalists to work more precisely. After a direct comment, "Stop, you hitting it, hold it in your hand. Pass it on the direction of the mouth (opening)," he sings, "Iron doesn't like Left-behind. Cut it short, short, let's go. Hold it like rice and its tying rope." The proverbs and their link are masterfully joined. "Iron doesn't like Left-behind" refers to the bush-clearing crew that works in a group to remove underbrush and fell small saplings on a rice farm: the slow worker is not welcome. The middle phrase is interesting, for one says "Cut it short, short, let's go" most often to encourage the women hoeing the soil for rice planting to keep with one another. The third phrase is the second proverb and it refers to the precision that is necessary as the rice is harvested; cutting one stalk at a time, one holds a rope to tie the bunch in the other hand in a most exacting manner.

Thus the three phrases refer consecutively to each of the major seasons of rice farming: clearing, planting, and harvesting. The first and the last are clearly proverbs of well-known use. These are linked by a more straightforward cue to form a well-rounded allusion for the instrumentalists. Kulung has used familiar language joined in his own aesthetic pattern to sing to his cohort performers. The care he wants in the music is the same tight cooperation people demand when they work en masse to clear the land and make a farm.

In Episode Three, Kulung comments on the musicians' performance that he so eloquently requested in Episode Two. He sings the proverb "A dancer doesn't stand outside, Then she has broken the law." Then he breaks into speech: "Initiated ones, thank you, thank you, thank you, thank you. That's the song, that's the song, that's the song, that's the song, that's the song." He has paid the players and singers a supreme compliment by comparing them to a dancer, for in this case the proverb refers to a really competent dancer. The proverb means that a really good performer must dance when the music is playing properly and will not resist the sound. To resist the sound will deny her gift. These performers are being told they are also skilled and have moved the performance to a new level of competence. This cue is a sign that Kulung thinks the music is moving beyond the tuning-in stage and becoming more focused on a kind of inner time.

This proverb also resonates with meaning for the plot. Spider has been brought to play the slit drum but in his concern for eating would rather not perform. He has no choice really as the food is circled around him. He needs to perform in exchange for the food and will be in trouble if he does otherwise.

Spider's dilemma is even more poignantly explained through a proverb sung a bit earlier in the episode:

> The Poro is on a person, the matter angers him.
> Night falls on him, the daylight bewitches him.

His plight is compared to the arbitrary and inarguable authority which the Poro secret society holds over people. Though he is upset about his required performance on the slit drum, he has no recourse in the matter. To say that night falls on him is another way to express that problems have come to him. The daylight itself bewitches him. He is a trapped person. This is a particularly tough spot for an individual in a society where most things are negotiable and are subject to being argued.

The pathos of spider is not without its comic element. For Spider cannot resist food, and the lengths he will go to to obtain food are well known in Kpelle folklore. Thus, with every bite he eats he entraps himself into the performance even more.

Nar. Ah, the food they are making! They are cooking rice again and packing it. And Wọi is lying in the sky.

Aud. What is he going to do?

Nar. When Spider is full, then Wọi will get out of the sky and get down. Then the war is ready.

Q. Don't lie to me.

Nar. Very close. I can't do that.
Wọi has now done it, Spider's rice. They set out the rice, eddoes, sweet potatoes, ripe bananas. All things they circle around him.

And thus we see Spider enclosed by his own undoing and weakness. Such a crisis is endlessly funny for the Kpelle; perhaps it so closely resembles the plight they often feel. The way his plight unfolds is also structurally similar to the way the episode unfolds. Circles move outward from the center of action. Whether it is Spider in the center or the epic audience, the expanding circles around them are the way life develops.

If each episode is a kind of moment to be built, Episode Six seems to be a moment whose expansion never really properly happens. The textures of movements are placed with the sound of the house moving, "zi, zi, zi," and the song of the gboto frogs in the swamps serenading the moving battle by singing Wọi's name repeatedly. But what is missing is both the description of the conflict of this episode and the embellishment of it with proverbs. These proverbs are the essence of the texturing. As one person who heard a playback of this commented, "He isn't able to pick the inside of the voice." It is this selection of the essences that makes the performance aesthetically pleasing and the moment fully expanded.

THE MOMENT IN CONTEXT

Ruth Finnegan mentions a range of events in Africa that feature musical performance—puppet shows of the Mande, masquerades, and epic enactment (1970:504). The performance of any event is determined by the intersection of a number of time dimensions. Fundamentally, the activities of the agricultural cycle may impinge. That is, during periods of heavy work, events are less frequent. Around harvest time, after the work is completed, events proliferate in many African communities. In areas where people work primarily in concessions as wage laborers, a proliferation of events may center around the monthly payday. The latter situation becomes more tied to the calendar and less to the social activities that serve to anchor life. Dale F. Eickelman comments on how the Bni Baṭṭu people of Morocco anchor the events of their lives.

> Events are sometimes remembered as occurring "before the sunset (prayer)," "at dawn," or "just before the market," but they are not ordered in a more abstract chronological sequence. Events like "Ahmed's death," "the famine," "the day the airplanes chased us," "before the Mahzen (government) came," "the sunup," "Hammu's wedding," and "when Sharef was small" are . . . largely unintelligible to outsiders since they can be translated only awkwardly into lineal concepts of time. (1977:44)

Thus, the very placement of events within the larger conception of time contains some fundamental differences from Western events which are commonly designated to occur on July 4 or December 25 or some other point of a linearly conceived calendrical sequence.

KINDS OF MOMENTS

Little research exists on the categorization by Africans of music events. J. C. Faris's work on the distinctions between "occasions" and "non-occasions" in Cat Harbour, Newfoundland (1973:112-24), is particularly relevant because his research involved not only elicitation of terms but observation of principles which produce the events, in order to better understand the creation and distinction between levels. Faris concluded that the Cat Harbour inhabitants' categories did not necessarily coincide with our notions, for a "concert" or a "supper" was not an occasion, but a "birthday" was. Through extended study he observed that an occasion was distinguished by its license for sanctioned deviance, whereas events known as non-occasions were not. With more research in Africa we could better know what Africans conceive to be events and what they do not. We know from Charles R. Adams's research (1974), for example, that the Basotho domain of performance groups music and games together.

Alan Goldberg, in his dissertation on Haitian vodun performance, comments that in looking at ritual events, and many musical events certainly are ritual, those scholars who stress the qualities of emergence and indeterminacy in the unfolding of the event "indicate that while social contradictions may be mediated or expressed in ritual, one of the effects of such expression may be to induce social change. . . . The deeper a ritual becomes, the more it captures the energies and involvement of the participants, making it capable of inducing change as well as ratifying tradition" (1980:4).

Understanding the complexities of event time and learning to live in its flow are difficulties for most non-natives conducting research in Africa. I vividly remember my own initiation to event timing in Kpelleland. Though I early developed a network of people who would inform me of musical events, I found it quite difficult, accustomed as I was to living by the clock, to determine when I should arrive at the scene of an upcoming performance. Kpelle acquaintances might tell me, "I hear they are going to play [perform] in Massaquoitaa for a death." If I pressed them for a time estimate, they would hesitate or offer some vague answer. My vivid memories, of early fieldwork especially, are of going to a location, only to arrive and find no evidence that a performance would occur, though people close to the deceased maintained that word had been sent calling the musicians. Hours passed as we waited, trying to keep busy by visiting with the local residents. The air in the town was invariably relaxed and unhurried. When, at long last, musicians came walking into town, a protracted negotiation often ensued concerning agreements and arrangements for the event. Characteristically, these talks threatened at several junctures to break down entirely and the result was, occasionally, no music making at all.

The clock time for the start of this performance was, within limits, quite variable. When the playing started depended to a great degree upon the quality of social interaction among the musicians and their hosts. As arrangements became more suitable to all, the performing time drew closer. Nevertheless, surprises were always possible and last-minute demands often threatened to destroy the bonds of understanding. The host or sponsor of the event was the most crucial party to negotiations with the musicians. The entire town population, however, often played a part, since their opinion of the group was often important to their support of the negotiations. If the musicians had a fine reputation, residents would urge a quick end to deliberations, for they anxiously awaited the music. I eventually learned not to ask "What time will the performance begin?" but "How are the negotiations proceeding?"

TIMBRE IN MOMENT

ACTION AND TONE COLOR

The emphasis on sound texture is pronounced in this epic. A part of each episode is devoted to describing sounds. In the fifth episode, as the bowl is carved, the very plot of the episode revolves around this play of sounds. Thus, what is introductory texturing in early episodes becomes the very centerpiece of the moment.

Sounds and movements are textured with the voice, and as the epic unfolds the voice shows that power. In Episode Five the voice carves bowls and creates things of great beauty. Later, in Episode Eight, the power of Wọi's voice is explored.

Nar. Wọi fixes everything with his voice. . . .
Wọi did things with just his mouth, with his voice.
If he said a person should die, that one died.
But, then, he doesn't do that because he is a chief.

Timbre, like transaction, appears to be a focus for Kpelle as well as for some other African musicians. Sue Carole De Vale, analyzing harp and vocal music of Uganda, has developed a graphic notation to highlight tone colors rather than pitch (1984:285-318). She describes the harp as playing with a "rough, percussive timbre" with a buzzing that requires a separate line of notation.

Just as De Vale uses a metaphor of weaving to explain her notation, Jeanette Harries finds it an apt image for Berber song in North Africa. One Berber poet compares himself to a woman weaving motifs in song as yarn is made into fabric (1973:144). Robert Thompson makes a similar analogy as he describes the narrow strip weaving of West Africa. A garment is constructed of up to a hundred strips joined into a single cloth.

> As multiple strips are sewn together by their edges, the major accents (weft-blocks) of one strip may be staggered in relation to those of an adjoining strip, with careful alignment of further elements in the same cloth preempting any assumption of accident and indeed confirming a love of aesthetic intensity through this form of special contrast. (Thompson 1983:208-209)

Thompson compares the staggering of accents in cloth to off-beat phrasing in music. And indeed the texture of music performance is not limited to sound textures or even visual textures that might result from a costume of such patterns as Thompson describes. Gerhard Kubik has long asserted that the visual kinesthetic component is critical as well. He notes that xylophonists in southeast Africa will often change the order of the keys on a loose log xylophone from one song to another. In doing so they can transfer the same or similar motor patterns to new key placement and get completely new combinations of sounds

(1972b:30-31). Moses Serwadda and Hewitt Pantaleoni also show how drumming and dancing are inextricably linked when they say, "In fact a drummer will indicate the dance motions sometimes as a way of explaining and teaching a [drum] pattern" (1968:52).

Text and Tone Color

A recent and interesting direction in rhythm analysis has turned toward the timbre and verbal text of rhythmic patterns. Francis Bebey once remarked, "It is scarcely an exaggeration to say that without African languages, African music would not exist" (1975:122). Many African musicians learn rhythm patterns, including the time line, through mnemonic phrases consisting of syllables that convey not only timing but also timbre. Koetting has commented that "the importance of sonority cannot be overemphasized" (1970:120).

The 12/8 standard pattern has been identified by a number of different phrases which are rendered in local languages. A few of the many that exist are shown in figure 11.

Figure 11. Comparison of Mnemonic Syllables

12/8	x .	x .	x x .	x .	x x .
Yoruba (Nigeria)	kọŋ	kọŋ	kọ-lọ	kọŋ	kọ- lọ (Kubik 1972a:169)
	kon	kon	ko -lo	kon	ko -lo (King 1960:52)
Bamenda (Cameroon)	kọ	kọ	kọ-ɣọ	kọ	kọ-ɣọ (Kubik 1972a:174)
Akan (Ghana)	koŋ	koŋ	ko -koŋ	koŋ	ko -koŋ (Kubik 1972a:174)

As Gerhard Kubik points out, the syllables can distinguish timbral subtleties to an extent that Western staff notation cannot. If we consider the first example in figure 11, Kubik indicates that although kọŋ and lọ are notated exactly alike as quarter notes in staff notation, the player of the kanango (hourglass drum) uses more energy to strike kọŋ than lọ. Lọ is a legato stroke. The ŋ means a silent pulse, providing a "complementary inaudible action unit" (Kubik 1972a: 170, 176).

Roderic Knight, in his study of Mandinka drumming in The Gambia, stresses the importance of timbre as opposed to duration when he points out that a drummer's skills are in part the ability to learn a rhythm as a "pattern of timbres" (1974:29). Knight goes on to explain the strokes as played for the Lenjengo recreational dance on the kutiridingo, a conical drum played with one stick and one hand (fig. 12). Kum is played with an open hand that bounces off the head. Ba is a damped stroke produced when the fingers hit the head and press it to lessen the vibration. Din is an open stick stroke. Da is a damped stick stroke (Knight 1974:28). Thus the syllables communicate a range of timbre much more complex than simple durational values.

Fig. 12. Kutiridingo Strokes

(6/8)	kum		ba	din		da
	K	•	B	D	•	d

(Knight 1974:28)

Among the Kpelle of Liberia, mnemonic syllables for the drum timbre and rhythm indicate, in addition, specific dance movements, the syllables differentiating movement and sound. For example, the mnemonic phrase keleŋ keleŋ represents forward shuffling from side to side, while se-ka-se-ke-kpa represents a complex step-and-turn pattern (Stone 1982:70).

The conclusion that timbral elements, so poorly communicated in staff notation, are essential to interpreting much of African music has resulted in several notational innovations. Serwadda and Pantaleoni have commented on the deficiency of Western notation symbols, which are "incapable of expressing the life blood of African drumming which is timbre" (1968:47). They suggest a new tablature type approach built from a prescriptive notation that indicates how the drum is to be struck in a kind of Labanotation. James Koetting has applied the TUBS notation to West African drum ensemble music.[46] Within the individual boxes of the graphlike structure, symbols characterize sonority by "representing the techniques used by performers to produce the pitch, loudness, tone quality, and carrying power of the sounds" (1970:127).

Syllables referred to by some ethnomusicologists as "nonsense" indicate rhythm. As Kubik points out, they are not properly termed "nonsense" at all, for they convey a great deal of meaning regarding how a rhythm is to be realized in terms of timbre and timing (1972a:169). That these mnemonic syllables derive from language should cause us to look more carefully at the use of language within songs. For example, when an ethnomusicologist concludes that a great deal of repetition occurs, the text that accompanies a song may not have been taken into account; within the text, a great deal of variety may exist. The evidence often lies in the text as analyzed by the folklorist and not the ethnomusicologist. The folklorist pays little attention to the music. That the texts of African performances are rich with clues about temporal organization is evident throughout Ruth Finnegan's volume *Oral Literature in Africa* (1970). The emphasis on timbre is evident in ideophones, employed not only in mnemonic devices but in song texts as well (Noss 1975:142-52). In Yoruba, for example, a high tone nasal vowel is often used to depict smallness while low tone shows

46. This system is not unlike one introduced by A. M. Jones to Zambian students some years earlier. "Each square represents the shortest unit of time used in a piece of music and one plots the notes accordingly" (Jones 1978:24).

large size or slow movement (Laṣebikan 1956:44). In Ewe and Gbeya, back rounded vowels are employed for ideophones indicating something dark or obscure (Samarin 1965:120).

Furthermore, phonemic tone, which is a part of many song texts, contributes to the overall temporal dimension. For, as Babalola points out in reference to Ijala, Yoruba hunter's poetry, specific patterns of speech tones may be repeated at irregular intervals, adding to the richness of the songs (1965:64-65). These speech tones may not be reflected in the melody, for a great many factors influence actual pitch.

In a related matter, in many areas of Africa instrumental or vocal parts are conceived not as inanimate sounds but as voices (Stone 1979; Zemp 1971; Berliner 1978:56). Thus, timbral subtleties are essential to the understanding of how all these "voices" interweave through time. Among the Shona of Zimbabwe, "musicians often refer to the B manual, which contains the mbira's lowest register, as the 'old men's voices,' the L manual, the middle register, as the 'young men's voices,' and the R manual, or highest register, as the 'women's voices'" (Berliner 1978:56). More specifically, individual keys have names and individually named voices, a phenomenon recognized in many other African communities as well.

VISUAL TEXTURE

The Kpelle create in epic an aural type of texture augmented with dramatic gestures. Since the epic pourer is kneeling, the hands and upper torso are foci of movement. The body is still bent forward as in the posture of a standing dancer, but the normal concentration of movement in the feet is shifted to the hands and arms. The mat is the stage area. Costume is not involved, nor is makeup. But the epic is not only sounded but expressed visually for a multimedia production.

In other parts of Africa, texturing may also involve visual displays of regalia. J. H. Kwabena Nketia describes the visual display element at the durbar event in Ghana, marking the climax of the forty-day ritual cycle honoring ancestor kings. The paramount chief exhibits, on this occasion, the regalia of his court in a splendid procession. Gold and silver ornaments abound, not only on the king but on members of the entourage. Of the music Nketia says,

> The drumming, singing and dancing during the procession keeps the procession alive. Different drum ensembles may be played simultaneously at different points within the procession. . . . As the music goes on, individuals may take turns at dancing in the open ring and the chief himself may grace the occasion by dancing to the music of the royal fọntọmfrọm drums. (1973:82)

The visual display has long been noted. Ibn Batuta, the great Arab traveler, set off in A.D. 1352 from Morocco, crossed the Sahara to Timbuktu, and traveled down the Niger (Jones 1957:8). Of the ruler of the Kingdom Mali, Batuta notes,

> When the Sultan is seated, from the lattice of one of the casement windows is thrown down a silken cord to which is attached a striped kerchief of Egyptian make; when the people see this, the drums are beaten and the horns are sounded. Each commandant has in front of him his men, with their spears, their bows, their drums, their horns (the latter made of ivory, or elephant tusks), and lastly their musical instruments made of reeds and gourds, which are beaten with sticks and make a pleasant sound.

As the Sultan processes to an open-air audience,

> In front of the Sultan go the singers holding gold and silver rattles; behind him are about three hundred armed slaves. The Sovereign walks leisurely. . . . Finally he slowly mounts the platform in the manner of a preacher mounting his pulpit: as soon as he is seated, they beat the drums, and sound the horn and trumpets. (Batuta 1858:403, 406, 411, in Jones 1957:8-9)

Whether aural, gestural, or regalia derived, these elements of the texture serve to expand a moment of music making and give it the play that people delight in. Much more than just the proper rhythm or pitches, these textures make a contribution to what is thought to be beautiful not only in the epic of Kpelle but in many other musical performances in various African societies.

CHAPTER 6

The Person in Epic

> **Wọi did things with just his mouth, with his voice. If he said a person should die, that one died. But, then, he doesn't do that because he is chief.**
>
> Wọi epic text

Central to the epic is the person, whether in the hero Wọi, in his people, or in the objects, plants, and animals that assume the attributes of persons. Musical sounds are "voices." Drums are equated with persons, and the parts of the drum are labeled with parts of the body: ear, body, foot (Stone 1982:91-92).

Of course this pattern is not unique to the Kpelle, for among the Lovedu of the Transvaal in Southern Africa the sacred drums (digọma) are referred to as gods and are mystically linked to the life of the queen and the well-being of her people (Krige and Krige 1954:67). The "person" becomes in many respects one of the metaphors for understanding music and, ultimately, culture in a number of areas of Africa. Marcel Griaule (1948), Germaine Dieterlen (1941), and Dominique Zahan (1960) point out the symbols connecting the person with social structure and cosmology. A more recent French volume, *La notion de personne en Afrique noire* (1973), includes an essay by Pierre Smith, "Principes de la personne et catégories sociales," in which he suggests that the correspondences between person and outer world can be extended to social divisions in the culture as well (Riesman 1981:8-9).

VARIETIES OF PEOPLE

The person constitutes a complex object in time. Alfred Schutz sets forth concepts that are suggestive for studying African societies: people are classified as consociates, contemporaries, or predecessors. He also presents some important distinctions for the understanding of the person in time. He maintains that on one hand a person lives in time, experiencing and acting. In this attitude a person lives in the present and directs action to the immediate future in what

Schutz terms a "vivid present." On the other hand, an individual understands himself in relation to his context only by reflection on what has taken place. In this second attitude, the person considers the past, even the just past. Thus, Schutz maintains that a person experiences time dynamically, living and experiencing a present moment, as well as reflecting on past moments (1973:172-79).

The Wọi epic is a capsule of reflection on the past which the Kpelle experience in the present. The Kpelle appear dynamically to reconstruct that reflection as existing in the present moment. In this way they build a reflection similar to that of James Olney's idea of "a creative figuration of the living present and a summary reconstruction of how the present came to be that which it is and that which it represents itself as being" (1972:264). In constructing a person through memory, for example, people rework and refigure the past to fit the present context. Time in such perspective is dynamic. For example, though the Wọi epic appears to be very old, Kulung refers to an airplane in one episode. The airplane belongs to Wọi and moves with all the attributes formerly given to Wọi's house. Thus, the house motion is called airplane movement but is otherwise quite the same.

All people grow older, never younger. Yet the interpretation of this fact can, in different societies, appear as something quite different altogether. For example, among some African peoples death means ascendance to ancestor status and is quite desirable. Wọi represents a preeminent ancestor and serves as a model for the Kpelle. He is part of that extended kin group that Igor Kopytoff maintains comprises "communities of both the living and the dead. The term 'ancestor' sets up a dichotomy where there is a continuum" (1971:129, 140), and in this Kopytoff is supported by James L. Brain (1973:122-33), even though Brain argues for African separation of these concepts.

The characters of the Wọi epic, whether they are a bow, a pumpkin, or a spirit, assume human qualities. Their particular attributes derive from their nature as an object or animal within Kpelle cosmology. Spider is clever but also greedy, a kind of archetype for the Kpelle personality. Axe cuts the tree with his special supernatural powers. Pumpkin can swell to enormous size to block the movement of the house. Anteater divines the future. These actions either aid Wọi in moving his house or hinder him. And these characters all live and act in a singular universe that unites humans, spirits, plants, and objects.

Mẹni-maa-fa, the lizard-monster spirit, is perhaps the most shifting of the characters. Lizard appears as a person to court Wọi's sister and marry her. Then when he reveals his true nature, she returns to Wọi. Enraged, Mẹni-maa-fa enlists the aid of Bat to retrieve her. A summary of the people and anthropomorphic characters indicates their affinity or enmity to Wọi (see fig. 13). The spirits here become enemies, as do many of the plants, while most of the people, animals, and objects are allies.

Figure 13. Characters and Attributes

Wọi —all powerful in battling foes

("-" = foes of Wọi; "+" = allies of Wọi)

People

+ wives —jealous one, who carves bowls with voice
—one who gives birth to all things
+ sister —married to Mẹni-maa-fa spirit
+ daughter —Maa-pu, waits to set fire to Bẹlẹ-Tree
+ sons —Zu-kpeei (older) —Wọi-boi (younger) —both sons attempt to cut down Bẹlẹ-Tree blocking house

Spirits

- Ɣele-lawọ —also bitter rattan plant
- Mẹni-maa-fa —Lizard
- Gemila —plucks out eyes

Animals

+ Spider —plays slit drum for music to forge iron
+ Tuu-tuu-Bird —pumps bellows for iron forge
+ Anteater —diviner
+ Poling-Bird —fights Gemila spirit
+ Squirrel-Monkey —accompanies Wọi to fight Ɣele-lawọ
+ Tsetse-Fly —accompanies Wọi to fight Ɣele-lawọ
+ Horse-Fly —accompanies Wọi to fight Ɣele-lawọ
+ Beetle —helps blacksmith to make needle for sewing Wọi's war clothes
- Bat —assaults house
+ Bull —belongs to Wọi, stolen by Mẹni-maa-fa
+ Bees —swarmed on the bull's horns

Objects

+ Bow
+ Arrow —with Bow, attempts to strike down Lizard
+ Bag —contains implements to help Wọi
+ Axe —cuts tree
+ Cutlass —helps cut tree
+ Double-edged-Knife —splits Pumpkin

Trees and Plants

- Bẹlẹ-Tree —obstacle to Wọi's house
- Koing-Tree —obstacle to Wọi's house
- Pumpkin —swells to block house
+ Koong-Leaf —serves as a trap for Bat, who is assaulting Wọi's house

LIFE TRAJECTORY

For musicians and people who perform and thereby create epic, biography is of some interest. Among the Kpelle, childhood is a time for attendance at events and learning about music through absorption.

Kulung, epic storyteller-singer, described his learning to perform epic as beginning when he was a small child. He listened to the epic performers, who were in those days quite numerous. Adolescence for Kulung brought the time of extended participation when he and his age mates learned the rudimentary dance and music skills necessary to become properly socialized Kpelle people. Following a rather intense period of music performance, particularly common during and following seclusion in the Poro society, Kulung was one of the select individuals who emerged to receive specialized training. He listened and watched carefully the epic performances of a local master. He then tried to perform on his own. He claimed that with careful observation he could reproduce an episode just heard. As a mature adult, Kulung became competent to perform on his own. He continued performing well past middle age, when most musicians usually defer to younger people, and was still performing when he died of alcoholism in his late fifties. He was thus an exceptional individual in Kpelle society.

If the skill of music rests with the young, the knowledge of musical practice—embodied in myths and oral history—resides with the elders. Though it may be the youth who do music, it is the old who know and contemplate it (cf. Murphy 1980). Thus, for an average Kpelle person (if any really exists) the biographical trajectory associated with physical change can be diagramed as in figure 14.

Involvement with music, in Kpelle terms, does not necessarily diminish with age, for knowledge and understanding are power and it is the elders who comprehend the subtleties of the performance and the layered references. In Kulung's case, late in his life he was both a performer and a knowledgeable elder and, as such, was somewhat of an anomaly (Stone 1984).

Figure 14. Musical Trajectory

The Kpelle

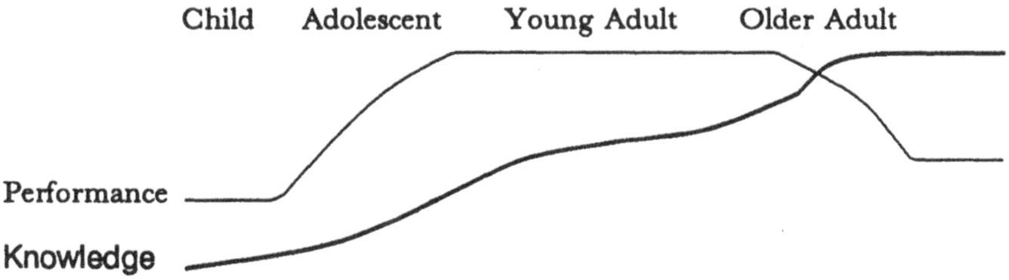

Child Adolescent Young Adult Older Adult

Performance

Knowledge

The lives of musicians elsewhere in Africa present a number of interesting dimensions. Though we do not have any published full-length life histories, we have extracts and summaries of the lives of individual musicians given to us in the works of Paul Berliner (1978), Charles Keil (1979), J. H. Kwabena Nketia (1973), and Alan P. Merriam (1973). David Ames concentrates on general profiles of musicians as a class, which provides some broad characteristics (1973).

The details revealed in the unfolding of particular biographies are crucial for understanding the social biographical path. For example, Nketia describes Kwame Tua, a musician who held a reputation among the Ashanti for using song as a weapon of criticism and insult. He lived an exciting life, first training to be a carpenter and trading in rum. He served both in the British-Ashanti war in 1900—on the side of the British—and in World War I in East Africa. Later he became a chief for a short time before being deposed. As Nketia's account concludes,

> Kwame Tua married about 30 wives, most of them daughters and grandchildren of chiefs, and had about 50 children. As a solo musician he always needed the support of a fellow artist. Two people collaborated with him: Amankwaa who played the bell, and Dwenti who played the second bell and sang the responses for him. He had six brothers and two sisters and was the second child in the family. (1973:95)

These details about his life indicate something of his relations to those around him and sharpen the picture we have of him.

Charles Keil recounts how Ikpamkor, a Tiv composer, wanted a birthday, supporting Keil's characterization of Ikpamkor as a man in search of the modern. Keil presents Ikpamkor's own words:

> I went and asked my parents. I asked them whether they could tell me the exact date of my birth. They said they did not know, for at that time there was no education and so they could not write it. They told me that Kpiato Adikpo was installed as chief then. . . . Then I went and searched the records for the date of Kpiato's installation and they told me that it was on the seventeenth of August, 1928. That was how I came to know my birthdate. (1979:106)

It is difficult to construct, from the various accounts, a typical biography. Paul Berliner does attempt to present some generalizations from the profiles he offers of Zimbabwean musicians. For many individuals, Berliner notes, the mbira was inaccessible to them when they were young. When they persisted, however, their interest was taken seriously and they were provided with instruction. Playing continued to be important to them because of the income they could derive. Some were able, for example, to earn their way through school (Berliner 1978:207-45). Dan Ben-Amos also cites the economic motivation for storyteller-singers to continue performing in Benin City, Nigeria (1972), though certainly not all African musicians earn such amounts. In many cases rewards are only token amounts of money.

The learning pattern varies also among African peoples. For the Hausa, the right to become a musician at all is inherited patrilineally (Ames 1973:152). Similarly, in areas where the musicians belong to a particular caste (Mali, Senegal), opportunities to learn are ascribed rather than achieved. A striking practice is the emphasis on learning through exposure to and absorption in musical performance (Nketia 1973:87). Children have many opportunities to attend music events from a very early age. They are present and part of village music making. A great deal of knowledge is gained in this way. Often only after considerable evidence of talent is formal instruction, frequently in the form of apprenticeship, carried out.

The relations of musicians to those around them are stereotypically difficult. Performers are often depicted as low in social rank but functionally high in importance (Merriam 1973:260; Ames 1973:152). My own research among the Kpelle contradicts this, for I have found musicians to be quite highly ranked. Those who had low social rank tended to be musicians who had largely abandoned their obligations to the village and ties to the land to become wanderers. Kulung was a case in point, for though he performed and knew much of the esoteric background of music, he had largely relinquished his tie to his local community. He was a highly regarded musician with relatively low status in his own community. In that sense he was not unlike Mrs. Zenani, a difficult ntsomi singer from southern Africa, of whom Harold Scheub says,

> Even her many detractors, those who dislike her personally, are silent, emotionally involved in the *ntsomi* image when she is in the midst of her performance; many of them participate against their wishes, taking their cues from this artist who has ultimate control over the production, and so they become psychologically and rhythmically a part of the performance. (1972:117)

Such accounts also reveal that musicians, particularly within the performance context, wield considerable power, and this force certainly influences the opinions held of them.

SPIRITUAL ASPECTS

The spiritual or supernatural aspect of a musician's life is an extremely crucial one. The liaisons, often very private, that occur between musicians and various ancestral spirits serve to enhance and better the quality of the musician's performance. Though Kulung does not speak openly of any tutelary spirit, he addresses this spirit repeatedly in the epic. When he does so it is always through song:

Episode 1

Oh, Maa-laa bring my voice, oh my people.
. . . Ee Maa-laa-kẹ-ma doesn't fool around.

Sun-falling, ee Maa-laa bring my voice.
Sun-falling, ee Maa-laa bring my voice.

Episode 2

Ee, Maa-laa bring my voice.
. . . Ee, what does Maa-laa-kẹ-ma say?

Episode 3

Sun-falling Maa-laa, keng-keree.
. . . Sun-falling Maa-laa-kẹ-ma, oh, keng keree.

Episode 4

Ee, Maa-laa-kẹ-ma, bring my voice.
Oh, Maa-laa-kẹ-ma, bring my voice.

When the audience challenges Kulung about the truth of a point in Episode Five he responds, "Sun-falling Maa-laa doesn't play, oh." In this he seems to challenge the audience by citing his higher supernatural authority. In Episode Six he seems to be commenting on the plot to the tutelary rather than directly requesting aid: "Sun-falling, Maa-laa-kẹ-ma, it's the fight going there."

As one son of a Shona mbira player in Zimbabwe told Paul Berliner,

> You see, we who play the mbira were chosen by the spirits to play. When we play, it is not just for music . . . it can bring rain. . . . Even these mbira themselves are not ours. They belong to the spirits and have been passed down to us. This one was made before my father was born. This other one that is being made for me, I will pass on to my children. (1978:235-36)

The musicians express the feeling that the spirits are a vital part of their musicianly life and its unfolding. Among the Akan of Ghana this means that musicians are accorded the status of sacred persons while performing (Danquah 1928:51, in Nketia 1973:93).

As musicians possess certain supernatural attributes, they may also pass these on in certain instances. In the case of an Akan singer in Ghana, as she lay on her deathbed she summoned her daughter and passed on her "quality of voice and her gift as a singer in her spittle" (Nketia 1973:87). Thus transition was achieved in a supernatural manner. In a case that Hugo Zemp recounts, a Dan musician in Ivory Coast was recruited not by another person but by spirits in a vision. While he was working at his loom one day two dwarf spirits appeared and commanded him to go and hang himself. Though he attempted to do so, some villagers rescued him. When they went to a diviner afterwards, he was told that unless he continued the family tradition of becoming a harp-lute player he was doomed to die. Thus he embarked on the career of a musician (Bebey 1975:20).

Warren d'Azevedo provides some detail concerning the relationship of the tutelary spirit (neme) of the Gola of Liberia. The spirit exists in a private and often secret relationship, complete with a covert code of conduct. Though such a relationship allows a performer to be extraordinary, it is fraught with considerable danger. The spirit may promise the human being success, but it will extract considerable personal sacrifice for its own selfish purposes. As d'Azevedo concludes,

> Because the neme relationship is one of precarious struggle between private and public values, between one's own self and a powerful seductive spirit, it is claimed among the Gola that the average person rejects any advances from jina. (1973:295)

The musician is thus placed in the position of participating in such a relationship if he or she anticipates success as more than a pedestrian performer.

The tutelary spirits can hardly be overemphasized, for they are, in a covert way, part of the musician's biography. His or her inner experience of music is shared intimately with this being. Thus, the musician is not really alone in the spiritual biography but rather shares it with contemporaries. The tutelary becomes a kind of shadow that accompanies the musician throughout his or her career. Without it, success is limited. With it, life becomes much more high-risk.

LIFE HISTORIES

Extended life history accounts may tell us something about how a musician places his own life in a time perspective. As Michael Agar defines it, a life history is "an elaborate, connected piece of talk presented in a social situation consisting of an informant and an ethnographer" (1980:223-39). The musician chooses in this setting how to present himself, what to tell and when to tell it, with the ethnomusicologist as audience. Our analysis of the life history attempts to decipher what the musician is trying to project in order to understand what we have been told. One part of this complex account is the temporal dimension.

The life histories obtained from Kpelle musicians reveal interesting sequencing. In no case did I receive a life history that could be characterized as chronological. Even when a musician began with an account of his youth, he jumped around in chronological time. Though I was never able to obtain a life history from Kulung, the epic singer, I give here a portion of the life history from Kao, master drummer from Gbeyilataa whom I have known over the past twelve years. (It was tape recorded and later transcribed and translated.) Kao, a handsome, sturdy man, pondered before speaking and then the words poured forth in an animated presentation. At the end of a section, he often sat back again in silent thought. One time, after some minutes of silence, my assistant, Zau, asked him what he was doing. He responded, "I'm walking in my mind."

I was born in Mopaitaa, Kanema. But I was in Yilataa when I reached puberty and got a wife who had the children here. But I stayed there, and I said, "I'm going to my brother." He is the only one—we can sit together and think of each other. That's why I went to him. I've spent two years in Pee. This is the second finishing here.

My mother's name is Mẹẹgọ. My mother's older sister we call her Atii, but her name is really Lepee. She's at Yilataa right now. My older brother's name is Kutu, his Kpelle name is Kpakoloi. He is the land's citizen. He's an important person in Pee.

I began playing the fẹ̀li [goblet drum] when I was a child. I began this work in Kwata. That's where we were when I started this work. It is near German Camp. That is the area where I was as I began to get big. I was a big boy before we came to Yilataa. I started that work [drumming]. Our father was called Mala-ɣale Tokpa. If you hear that in Kpelle from a Zọkọlẹ [northern Kpelle] person then that is a goblet drum player. As a young boy I took old cans and hit them. And it was so mọ tọ tọ tọ [passage of time]. Where we were, I learned to play the drum for the horn playing ensemble. I really played the fẹ̀li in Kwalataa. And it stayed that way mọ tọ tọ tọ. I was now a big small boy. I was really a fẹ̀li player.

The reason I am no longer playing, the reason is that I am getting mature. It is not because of money. The playing I do, my children pass under my feet and I feel ashamed. It isn't because I am too great a person to play. It is two years since I resigned from playing. I began in playing for horn ensembles. A baby monkey sat on my shoulder as I played. There is where my drum playing came from. Having played fẹ̀li so long and growing up it is difficult for my hands to run away [lose my skill]. I am sitting here and telling you I no longer play. Two years have passed. I tell you my understanding is in my stomach and in my hand. But if you want me to record, that which I will play, you will take it. If you didn't believe in me and I in you, I wouldn't have come. . . .

My father did not teach me drumming. But what your father does you can do a little of. Drumming and drumming for horns is different. They showed it to me and I was able to do it. I knew I was able to do it when the performance fell [began] and they gave me the drum. When we played we went to distant towns such as towns all in the area where Camp #1 and Camp #3 are [Salala Rubber Corporation]. I kept playing until one woman caught a love name on me. She cooked a really fine meal, but I was a child and the big people ate it and gave me the message. The woman's name was Gbẹẹ. She was in a town to which we traveled.

I have two wives. My wife whose children were sitting here is called Kwii-talọọ-ya. Her father is Kẹkula Gbolo-kpuai. He is in Yilataa right now. My wife is in Pee. My other wife, she is called Kinẹ-goo-saa. If it works out and we have sweet conversation, then she will be my wife. I married Kwii-ta in the church in Yilataa. Her first child is the one I think you recorded. It is

> good in traditional Kpelle society to have two wives that get along. A woman is our rib. If a woman mistreats you and you mistreat her, sadness will befall you.
>
> If something happy happens to me, and I have a drum, if it is voiced, I will play the drum complete. If you have a child and you are a performer, then people talk and say, there is his child dancing, and he is dancing. But I can do performing. When I'm in Gibi, my older brother doesn't drink cane juice, doesn't smoke cigarettes, he doesn't use snuff. He is very humble. He does not want drunkards, but he would not stop me.
>
> The drums all belong to Yilataa. If I go someplace, I cannot take them, they belong to the town. But I made some of them and only if someone tells me that I do not own them would I know that I did not own the town drums. But I own all the drums. I carved some and raised the heads. The town owns the drums and I cannot take them from them because the town is a family town. (Stone 1975:61-62)

The very first paragraph constitutes a précis of Kao's life. He tells where he was born, where he moved to and first married. Throughout the narrative, he returns to fill in details of this thumbnail sketch. The sentence "But I stayed there and I said, 'I'm going to my brother'" condenses a great deal. For it encloses a major disagreement that Kao had in Gbeyilataa which caused him to move to Pee, the region where he had lived as a child, even though he was the leading musician and orchestrator of the performing group in Gbeyilataa. The paragraph concludes with his observation that he had spent the last two years in Pee and brings us up to the present.

Kao proceeds to explain his family, naming his mother, her older sister, and his brother, all significant individuals in his life. An account of how he learned to play the fẹli follows. Then he discusses why he no longer plays, only to return in the following paragraph to a little more elaboration of his learning years. Next we hear of his two wives. Again he returns to the theme of not playing but rationalizes that it is not for lack of skill. Finally we have a discussion concerning ownership of the fẹlis in Gbeyilataa. Though the life history continues at some great length, this excerpt gives us enough information to see the difficulty in discerning a chronological pattern. Kao moves easily about through time, switching from past to present and back again. There is also no doubt that Kao, or anyone giving a life history, is presenting his life as he wants it to be seen and in ways that he has learned are appropriate. It is up to the researcher to probe the reasons for such a presentational thrust and style.

We are given no in-depth biographies of individual characters in Wọi epic. We come to see them from their present existence. They are not presented in the context of well-established genealogies, even as the Kpelle do not characteristically place themselves within long genealogies.

As more such life histories are recorded, we will know about the overall temporal dimensions that exist in them. At present, no conclusions are possible, only speculations that such patterns might be of interest. Nevertheless, we can see that the avoidance of linear progression in life history is not so different from the pattern of epic episodes. For after all, isn't the epic a life history being narrated by someone else? This life history is that of the archetype Kpelle person, a life history in which all share, for all are descended from this person. The mosaic style of construction obtains in the epic and the life history alike, and actions are linked more by association than causation.

CHAPTER 7

The Epic in Local Life

Time goes slowly in the village, quickly in the forest.

Lele people of Zaire
(Douglas 1954:4)

All days are not equal.

Taxi motto
(Chernoff 1979:163)

The animation of performing Wọi epic is created, to a great extent, by the web of village and community activity in which the Kpelle live. What makes this epic exciting is the way it plays off of the ordinary and everyday ways of doing things.

The Kpelle order time from local event landmarks rather than from just physical, personal, or clock marks (cf. Lewis and Weigert 1981:433). To better understand the depths of the Wọi epic we can note the outlines of this local time reckoning. The ordering of local life is both hinted at in the Wọi epic itself and reflected in the lives of people who perform it.

LIFE CYCLE

Each person's life is influenced by the social definition of the life cycle. Each society defines certain life stages or important "moments" (Turner 1967:7) and accompanying rites that achieve transition between stages. Such interpretations affect and alter the way a person's biography is ordered. They also "mark changes in ties of blood, marriage, cash, political control, and in many other ways" (Turner 1967:7).

The Wọi epic does not explicitly feature the life-cycle landmarks. Rather, it makes fleeting reference to them, and the audience, familiar with their details, is reminded of them. In Episode Two, where Wọi's wife gives birth to living things, the simple phrase "just cut a road" reminds the audience of the path cut to an enclosure away from the village where a woman delivers a child and of all the attendant rituals of that place. In the first episode Kulung, in the song, sings "Oh, I'm the one who gave your feast," referring to the feast associated with initiation into the secret society. The feast for Spider in Episode Three compares his plight at not being able to resist the food and then being compelled to play music to a person in the Poro and the tremendous force of authority in that situation. "The Poro is on a person, the matter angers him/ Night falls on him, the daylight bewitches him." The fifth episode, that of the jealous wife carving bowls with her voice, features quite forcefully a central problem in marriage maintenance in Kpelle society. Though enemies are slain, the issue of death and mortality is studiously avoided throughout the epic. Connection to spirits is constant, as Kulung calls on his tutelary spirit frequently and indirectly emphasizes his supernatural aid.

For the Kpelle, the initiation into Poro or Sande is prerequisite to adulthood and therefore critical to any further movement within the life cycle. Reference to the feast of initiation by Kulung recalls for the audience a time when the initiate returned from the extended physical separation required by the secret society, a time of death of the old person and birth of the new adult. Kulung also refers to the temporal transition that characterizes the lack of status that the initiate experiences on the way to becoming an adult. While the individual is undergoing initiation, a common activity involves the communication of essential sacred features of the culture. Victor Turner identifies this as reducing the culture to recognizable components, recombining things into monstrous patterns, and reordering things in ways that make sense for the new status of the neophytes (1967:106).

Music performance is frequently deemed essential to life-cycle ceremonies. For example, at the beginning of Ndembu initiation ritual, three rivers are dug and filled with white, red, and black water. Neophytes are enlightened, partly through riddling songs, as to what each river signifies, and music in a playful way reveals meanings important to Ndembu culture and the neophytes' understanding of it (Turner 1967:107).

Among the Kuranko of Sierra Leone, much of the activity in initiation rituals inculcates the belief that in order to sustain individual life one must observe a respect for customs prescribed by the "first people" or ancestors. Life is sustained by attending to the elders. Furthermore, with initiation forming an important divide in the life stages, a person then moves gradually toward the ancestors and the past becomes a more central part of life (Jackson 1977a:17). For the Kpelle, Wọi becomes a proto-ancestor and well as the anchor character of the epic.

Specific numbers are associated with certain life-cycle events. Among the Mende of Sierra Leone, as among the Kpelle of Liberia, the number four is associated with male and the number three with female. Interestingly, among the Hausa three is associated with male and four with female, a pattern opposite from that of the Mende and Kpelle. Other patterns also emerge, with nine associated with male and seven associated with female among the Peda of Benin, and five associated with a male and four with a female among the Bakoko (Bril 1979:367-76).

Among the Kpelle, these numbers are used to calculate life-cycle events. At birth, a male Kpelle child is kept secluded four days and a female child three days; and at death, the feast marking departure of the spirit occurs the fourth sunrise after a man is buried and the third sunrise after a woman is buried.

Although it may be tempting to say that durational time can be roughly estimated by life-cycle events, such estimation can be misleading from the point of view of a number of African peoples. Among the Kpelle, where young people enter the Poro or Sande seclusion for a period, physical puberty may not coincide with social puberty. Within any single Poro group the initiates may range from the age of six years to twenty years or more. Furthermore, though the young men's Poro lasts four years, initiates enter at a number of different points during the four-year period. Among the Tiv, where age-sets are formed when the members are about twenty years old, an interesting conception of time exists. The Tiv told Paul Bohannan that all members of the age-set were born in the same year. Though one might conclude that an age-set is formed every year, careful study shows that an age-set is formed every three years. Still, the Tiv hold that all members were born in the same year. One is forced to conclude that the reference here is not to the durational aspect of the year (Bohannan 1953:258).

For the Karimojong each age-set is created of those men who have taken part in initiation ceremonies within a single five- to six-year period. Then five age-sets combine into a generation-set (cf. Hamer 1970). These groups serve to provide a ranking system within a group of herding people.

> The enclosure (*akiriket*) which is the physical center for every ritual is a microcosm of the age organization, showing individuals grouped with their coevals and distinguished collectively as seniors and juniors, and the course of events in every ritual is a serial display of age units in action in the roles appropriate to their standing. The members of the senior generation-set, by virtue of their age, stand closest to the division of natural and supernatural which is crossed by death. (Dyson-Hudson 1963:392)

While we can search for a reflection of these sacred numbers in performance details of the Wọi epic, they do not seem to be present. What is sacred and ritual in the epic does spring from these numbers associated with the life cycle.

Among the Kpelle, the entire initiation activity is critical to understanding performance in general. First of all, the initiates, both boys and girls, acquire skill in dance, particularly while they are secluded. Second, once the initiates emerge from seclusion, they are often featured performers at public entertainment events until the next group of initiates arrives several years later. They become a ready corps of performers and the village judges their skill with considerable attention to the details of execution. Whether they will perform as solo performers later depends upon the level of competence they exhibit. But following seclusion, most individuals perform in public for some period of time. Thus the time of initiation is one of heightened participation by most individuals in the music making. The corps of ready musicians that Kulung finds to assist him with performing Wọi epic exists as a result of their specific training within the secret society and the broad knowledge of performance principles they possess.

Other African peoples also associate musical performance skills with maturation. The kotè-tlon musical drama performance of the Bambara in Mali, for example, is an event linked to young men and the realization of personhood (Brink 1981:4). Through challenge of the elders in sanctioned ways, they achieve their adult status.

Kpelle people are often reminded of their initiation period when singers shift into the special nasal timbre that is considered appropriate when singing of things from the secret societies. And Kulung does this at key points throughout the epic.

The Wọi epic pays no attention to the act of marriage, in consonance with Kpelle lack of emphasis. But the institution of marriage receives considerable focus in the fifth episode, the jealous wife. Marriage among some other African peoples is marked by elaborated musical performance. The courtship phase among the Luo of Kenya includes oigo songs performed as young girls travel to meet a group of young men. When the girls arrive, the young men join the ensemble with their reed flutes.

Weddings among the Hausa, on the other hand, call for teams of maroka, or "praise" singers, who are the main recipients of the expensive gifts given on these occasions (Finnegan 1970:102). Among some of the Zambian peoples, a young man must sing a song he has composed at his wedding (Jones 1943:11). A Ganda girl about to be married may sing this song of farewell marking her change in status.

> Oh, I am gone,
> Oh, I am gone,
> Call my father that I may say farewell to him,
> Oh, I am gone.
> Father has already sold me,
> Mother has received a high price for me,
> Oh, I am gone. (Sempebwa 1948:18)

Among the Kpelle, marriage is an event marked by a series of token exchanges and discussions; otherwise, music performance is quite absent. Even birth, when the father might hire a group to perform, is likely to engender more performance.

On the occasion of weddings and other formal gatherings throughout Africa, praise singing often involves the recitation of lineages, though this is not typical for the Kpelle, nor is lineage recitation embedded in Wọi epic. As Judith

T. Irvine details those genealogies for the Wolof of Senegal, they appear to be a closer representation of the historical past than those of the Nuer, Luo, or Tiv—the latter genealogies appearing more as a projection of present-day political relationships upon the past. Thus, links to the past become important, for they serve, as Irvine suggests, to perpetuate the caste system. Part of one sung lineage follows:

> Yatma Fandag Aram Kodde, Matar Mamur Aram Kodde, Fakumba Aram Kodde your ancestor, they are related through both mother and father.
>
> Fandag Aram Kodde is [married] at the Samb household; she is there Yatma Fandag, and Masamba Fandag; Ndiaga Samb [praise-name for the Ndiaye family, chiefs of the village] sent [her] to go there [to marry a Samb].
>
> Fakumba Aram Kodde was at the village of Ker Mamaram; she had there Makhet Fakumba; Makhet Fakumba your ancestor had there Mokhuri Makhet; she is the Mokhuri Makhet who is the mother of Masamba Ngone, the lord of the village. (Irvine 1978:659-60)

As this lineage is presented it is recited predominantly in the present tense, with movement between the past and the present. Though some African peoples like the Kpelle do not emphasize genealogy of any depth, many do place people in relation to other people and these relationships are emphasized in song texts. Names are often an index to these relationships and the insertion of a person's names into performance is ubiquitous.

> Wọi-boi, Wọi-boi, Wọi is in the distant sky.
> Wọi's child is Zu-kpeei.
> . . . Zu-kpeei's younger sibling is Wọi-boi.

Many Africans maintain active communication with ancestors. An important means of conversation is through sacrifice, an act that helps to transcend not only space but also time. The belief is strong that one's well-being is tied to keeping the indirect dialogue open with those of the past (Jackson 1977b:125-26). In Wọi epic, communication with spirits who are called to attend the performance is ever present in the singing of Kulung.

In many areas, death also calls for performance so that an individual might efficaciously move to a new status. The Senufo funeral in Ivory Coast first and foremost assures the continuity of relationships between the world of the living and the world of the spirits (Glaze 1981:149).

> The measure of a man or woman's life is expressed both qualitatively and quantitatively in the design of the commemorative funeral. A long life characterized by numerous attainments and a proliferation of structural social relationships will be reflected directly in the commemorative funeral by length, elaboration and richness of texture and detail, and the number of participating individuals and groups. (Glaze 1981:153)

Funeral performance is the one kind of event that often continues in a community when the heavy work season, for example, has largely ended other types of music performance. Among the Kpelle, for example, wailing begins at the announcement of a death and is followed by ensemble performance of entertainment music until burial. Then, three days after a woman's burial and four days after a man's burial a death feast is held—those sacred numbers attending maleness and femaleness throughout life. If the farm work is too urgent, or if the family does not have the resources to have a proper feast, they can respond as I observed one family do. This group marked the dawn of the death feast with a proper sacrifice of a chicken and firing of a gun at the grave. This marked the beginning of the death feast. They then suspended further activities of the feast until such time as they could properly entertain the assembled relatives. Thus, durational time, halted when the feast began, simply did not proceed any further. When it did resume some months later, the proper closing markers ended the entire affair.

Among the Akan of Ghana, funeral dirges are composed and simultaneously performed without accompaniment during the public mourning phase of a funeral, following the preparation of the corpse. As Nketia points out, the Akan say, "One mourns one's relations during the funeral of another person" (1955:2). In this way, past deaths become part of any single death in a social abstraction.

Sjaak van der Geest suggests that death is a prominent theme in the texts of Akan highlife songs, where he noted that thirty-one of one hundred texts commented on the subject (Geest 1980:145-74). To offer these examples should not imply that death is observed to the same extent among all African peoples. Robert Thornton notes that, among the Iraqw of Tanzania, funerals are not important occasions of ceremonial observance. In fact, he says, the Iraqw conceive of death as involving no absolute change and no process of degeneration (1980:81).

When a child dies, the normal observances may be altered. Such observances may include a funeral conducted in silence and ritual characterized by symbolic actions reversing the birth process, as the Venda people do with a view to reordering the social world and restoring life (Schutte 1980:257-63).

Death can be muted in a number of ways. The Yoruba, for example, believe that certain children, noted for their physical resemblance, are reincarnations of deceased ancestors. The Yoruba also celebrate, during the annual Egungun festival, the return of the ancestors to earth. The ancestors express themselves through the masked dancers; the human dancer is merely a medium for the soul of the deceased, the dancer speaking in a special guttural voice to show this other form (Lawal 1977:59).

The Wọi epic is interesting for its notable avoidance of death and its stress instead on power and continuity. In that respect it contrasts with the usual Kpelle elaboration of this part of the life cycle.

The person living in time participates in music throughout a lifetime. This life is ordered in ways that do not necessarily give superordinate status to chronological time. The life cycle among the Kpelle and in other parts of Africa cannot be equated with similar notions of growth, maturation, and decay, for death, for example, implies movement to ancestorhood, and there is increasing stature in the community with age. In many areas of Africa elders are more revered than they are in the West. Furthermore, initiation is very much a death and rebirth process in those areas where there are special initiation ceremonies. Time in the life cycle takes on a complex character, and some peoples interpret even demise of the body to be birth itself into a new status. Whatever the individual experience in time, it must be related to certain interpretations of the life cycle by the various African peoples. The Wọi epic contains more reminders than details of life-cycle events. It places importance on the beginnings of all things and the continuity of all things without pointing out everything that is part of that continuity. The paramount place of initiation is assumed by the oblique references to the authority of the Poro. And in the end, the epic becomes more an abstract expression than a realistic portrayal of the Kpelle life cycle.

LOCAL EVENTS

Time in local life is located in and defined by a group of people. People define actions in time in relation to what other people in a group are doing. Life is regulated by points such as "Tolbert's government," "Zau's death," "market day," or "before dawn." The points represent isolates of shared experience meaningful to a group of people who interact in reference to them. These people may be able to relate them chronologically in a linear manner, but such ordering is not necessarily the most important emphasis.

The Wọi epic nicely illustrates this reliance on social actions to organize time. The narrative, predominantly in the present tense, shows how the war happens when the events warrant it. Kulung, in reference to Spider, says in Episode Three, "He will eat it and play the Slit-Drum. When he is full, then the war has started up." The war beginning depends on Spider's activities. Later on in the same episode, Kulung shows how they depend on Wọi as well. "Wọi said, 'Then sew my clothes. As soon as I've put them on, we will fight.'"

A considerable part of life in the local community incorporates calendar time—the time-reckoning concepts for days, weeks, months, and years. Research on African societies clearly indicates the dependence of these ideas in Africa upon social interaction and social events. One of the most significant and longstanding analyses in this regard in Africa comes from E. E. Evans-Pritchard. In his study of the Nuer (1940), his categories of "oecological time" and "structural time" both derive, in large part, from social action. Though under oecological time the two main seasons *tot* and *mai* relate to the rainy and dry seasons, they also relate to a cluster of social activities. Thus, the Nuer go to *tot* in a certain place rather than going to a certain place in *tot*. They do not travel *when* the season arrives. Rather, it arrives by coincidence when they travel

(1940:99). Across the continent, in West Africa, Paul Bohannan quotes the Tiv as saying, "The first harmattan comes when we cut guinea corn" (1953:255). The season does not serve pivotally to order the activities of either the Nuer or the Tiv calendar.

Evans-Pritchard also notes: "The calendar is a relation between a cycle of activities and a conceptual cycle and the two cannot fall apart, since the conceptual cycle is dependent on the cycle of activities from which it derives its meaning and function" (1940:100). He goes on to explain that Nuer, like the Kpelle, do not use the names of months to any great extent. They refer, rather, to the activity to place events. In a similar vein, structural time is reckoned in structural distance. "Any kinship relationship must have a common point of reference on a line of ascent, namely a common ancestor, so that such a relationship always has a time connotation couched in structural terms" (Evans-Pritchard 1940:106).

Evans-Pritchard's ideas set an important direction for examining the reckoning of African concepts of time, for he indicates a nondurational pattern that depends upon social relationships, a pattern that has been more richly detailed in subsequent studies.

The Kpelle also conform to this anchoring of time in social activity. The very beginning of an epic performance can be predicted more by the quality of people's talk and feelings than by any watch ticking.

Periodic events may serve to maintain local ordering of time and the quality of social interaction. The Ashanti hold the Odwera ceremony once a year. The first of the harvest is offered to the ancestors as the chief leads a musical procession to the graves. In one of the prayers, a priest says, "the edges of the year have met . . . may there be peace during the present chief's reign" (Busia 1954:203-204). The Kpelle similarly compare the year to a circular fence which encloses a farm. In fact, the name for fence (korang) and year is identical.

The "growth, decline, and renewal of chiefship provides the central temporal movement that guides and orders ecological time" among the Bashu of Zaire. That is, when the chief is in control, ritual control exists, ecological time flows smoothly, and crops flourish. When a chief dies, the flow of time slows, and only with the installation of a new chief is the ecological dimension once more energized (Packard 1981:31-32). The initiation of a new chief, *mwami,* takes place at sunset at a new moon and with a separation from the homestead. In the bush he begins movement to the new status much as a bride moves from her home to that of her husband or as a young man enters the bush at sunset for circumcision (1981:35-36).

The Lovedu of Transvaal establish a year by beating the sacred drums and visiting the graves of the royal ancestors. They appeal to the spirits for rain and thank them for the harvest by beating the drums at important moments in the agricultural year, indicating points of interaction with supernatural beings (Krige and Krige 1954:66).

DAILY TIME RHYTHMS

The daily rhythm of time in African communities directly affects music making. The day versus night concept, for example, is important, for music is often considered a more appropriate form of sound at night. The Wọi epic is appropriately performed at night, and not during the day when work is to be done. The exception to this is a day like market day when people suspend their usual work to meet for social and economic interchange in a prearranged town. Among the Lele of Zaire, drumming is legitimate at night, while other day noises are forbidden (Douglas 1954:1-26). Many African peoples divide the day by the position of the sun in the sky (Paulme 1940:166; Evans-Pritchard 1940:100; Jackson 1977a:122). As Evans-Pritchard comments, among the Nuer the transition periods yield richer terminology, and between 4:00 and 6:00 A.M. there is more differentiation than for the rest of the day (1940:100). Kenneth Little notes that among the Mende of Sierra Leone, ceremonies and sacrifices often take place at dawn, which is considered to be a time of increased vigor (1954:117; cf. Wagner 1954:51).

In some areas, daily time divisions are marked by specific types of music performance. In the Fon court in Dahomey there is a complex cycle.

> There is a concert of *dogba* music before the king arises in the morning, and this goes on until about 9:00 A.M. The musicians go round the palace as they play. The music of *hanhye* follows this for an hour and a half. *Gbolo* follows and is played until midday, when the reciters of praise poetry take over. Later in the day the orchestras *goke* and *agbadja* are played in succession. Trumpets are played at nightfall, and the round ends with the music of *ako*. (da Cruz 1954, as quoted in Nketia 1971)

The junctures of daily time that the Kabyle of Algeria distinguish are "when the sky is red," "the time of the first prayer," or "when the sun touches the earth." Thus, where Islam is part of the cultural fabric, the Muslim practice of praying five times a day and sounding the call to prayer from the mosque is integrated with positions of the sun.[47] But even with these prayers, which Westerners designate numerically, linear time is not paramount. As Pierre Bordieu explains,

> The islands of time which are defined by these landmarks are not apprehended as segments of a continuous line, but rather as so many self-enclosed units. . . . Each of the temporal units is an indivisible block juxtaposed to the others. (1963:59)

47. Michael Jackson claims the Muslims in the Kuranko area pray four times a day (Jackson 1977a:22).

In support of Bordieu's assertion, Dale Eickelman comments that the Bni Baṭṭu of Morocco punctuate the day by "point-like" prayers. The people see these prayers as related, but not as orderly divisions to be used for quantifying time (Eickelman 1977:44). Thus, what might be quantifiable time or linear progression from a Western researcher's perspective is interpreted in an alternative way by Africans, in this latter case by an Arabic-speaking group.

The day, taken as a whole, appears to be a prime focus in Africa. Indeed, Thomas Beidelman notes that the East African Kaguru most frequently refer to the day in time references, "today" being most prominent (1963:13). Such a focus is consistent with a desire for present-centeredness. This preference in the Wọi epic means that there is a lack of indication about any other time period. Wọi's actions take place in the here and now and any description in the past tense is of the immediate past. Phrases to describe time passing are also lacking. The exception is in the narrator's reflective song where he often sings "sun-falling" to bring a sense of urgency not to the narrative of Wọi but to his plight as a performer. The passage of time affects only his world and not Wọi's. In Episode Six he enhances the phrase by singing, "Sun-falling, sun that doesn't wait until noon." Finally, in Episode Eight he sings, "Sun-falling, they are calling us again at night." In this he means that he has done the equivalent not only of a day's work but of a night's as well in his performance.

WEEKLY RHYTHM

A cycle of days differentiated one from another and forming a unit takes a number of forms in Africa. The Tiv and Dogon, for example, have—or had—a five-day cycle that can be equated roughly to a week (Bohannan 1953:255; Paulme 1940:298). The Kuranko of Sierra Leone and the Abron (Akan) of Ivory Coast maintain a seven-day pattern (Jackson 1977a:22; Niangoran-Bouah 1964:9-26). The Akan calendar is a synthesis of a six-day week, which is still observed in northern Ghana, with a seven-day week that may have been brought with traders. "When the six-day week is counted side-by-side with the seven-day week it takes a total of forty-two days to reach all combinations" (Bartle 1978:82). The Akan characterizations of the six- and seven-day week are given by Bartle (1978:81-82) as in figure 15.

Frequently the days are named according to which town holds market on a particular day. In many areas the market rotates within a nucleus of nearby towns, moving to a different town each day and back to the first at the beginning of the next cycle. The Kpelle word for "week" is lọkuu, "feast of the market." With such a localized system of naming, it is clearly possible, as Paul Bohannan points out, that the same day of the week will be known by different names depending on where one is located (1953:255).

Among the Abron, the names of the days of the week are also used to derive names for children. A boy born on Sunday is called Kwassi, while a girl born on the same day is known as Kossia (Niangoran-Bouah 1964:12).

The case can be made in many areas that traditional time-reckoning does

Figure 15. Akan Days of the Week

Six-Day Week

1. *Fo* Council day (passing sentence): judgment day
2. *Nwuna* Sleep (death) day; funerals day; covered day
3. *Nkyi* Behind (hate) day, destroyed day
4. *Kuru* Town (i.e. political) day; royal day
5. *Kwa* For nothing day
6. *Mono* Fresh (starting) day

Seven-Day Week

1. *Dwo* Monday, Quiet (peace) day; calm
2. *Bena* Tuesday, Birthday of ocean; heat, boiling, cooking
3. *Wukuo* Wednesday, Birthday of spider (reverse or mortal version of God)
4. *Ya* Thursday, Birthday of Earth (a woman); power
5. *Afi* Friday, Fertility; (in some Fante states, birthday of Earth)
6. *Mene* Saturday, Birthday of Supreme or Sky God
7. *Kwasi* Sunday, Underday

not focus on the days of the week. Therefore, as Eickelman says of the Bni Baṭṭu,

> Time reckoning in terms of the days of the week does not come easily to most tribesmen. They usually pause and reconstruct how many days have elapsed since the last market or remain to the next. This is the case even though all the days of the week except Friday . . . and Saturday . . . are simply numbers in sequence. (1977:43)

The day of market in any town is frequently the occasion for musical performance. On this day a considerable influx of people into the town brings a ready audience. After people have sold their produce and bought their tobacco, cloth, or salt, they often appreciate an opportunity to enjoy entertainment. I have seen solo musicians as well as larger ensembles perform. In some towns, radios, record players, and movies provide the music rather than live ensembles. In Totota, Liberia, in 1975-76, an itinerant movie projectionist showed East Asian martial arts, Indian, or American films each market day. The market women, and others, relaxed in the evening with this modern form of entertainment. Musically, market day could often be counted upon as a high point in activity. Indeed, in towns that are normally deserted during the day, when people go to wage labor or farm work some distance away, market day is a bustling contrast to all the other days of the week. Furthermore, since communication is facilitated at a market, arrangements for an upcoming performance are often made on market day. Market day is thus a crucial node to much music making, either as an occasion for actual performance or as a time to negotiate a future occasion.

MONTHLY RHYTHM

The month is reckoned in many areas of Africa according to the phases of the moon, a symbol in Nilotic cosmology, for example, of women, the human menstrual cycle, and the regeneration of life (Burton 1981:445). With a lunar type of calendar, the months are a few days shorter than in the solar calendar. Many peoples name these months. Among the Kpelle one must designate which calendar one has in mind, for official government uses the Gregorian calendar. The Kpelle hold a general but not complete consensus for the indigenous names of the months, which are ordered by lunar reckoning. The names, as given by some informants, are listed in figure 16. Thirteen names have been included because several people indicated that number.

Significant in the names of the months are those that express sound qualities. Whether the leaves are crunching, birds singing, or the wind blowing, the propensity to note sound qualities that we noted in the epic is also present here.

Figure 16. Kpelle Months

1. *gwęlę-yaloŋ-nee*— "the mother cold month." The month with the coolest evenings.
2. *nyeŋ-nyeŋ* — the onomatopoeic sound of leaves that crackle underfoot as one walks.
3. *vuu-laye*— the sound of cold winds that blow through the forest.
4. *dęniŋ* — "leaving." The act of growing new leaves that dropped earlier.
5. *maa-kpore*— means that there is only a small amount of rice life in storehouses.
6. *kali kara* — "hoe grass." The time of small weeds in the farm that can be taken out with a hoe.
7. *luę-luęi* — "mist." Common form of rain at this time.
8. *kpǫyǫǫi* — "mushroom soaked." If there is a lot of rain this mushroom emerges.
9. *manai* — contraction for "ɓa namui" (rice owner). Hunger is common now and there is always someone who claims to be the owner of rice.
10. *danai* — "there's some in my mouth." Rice is ripening everywhere and when someone offers you food, you can always answer with this response.
11. *ŋwee* — onomatopoeic voice of a bird that appears.
12. *bǫrǫŋ-kpalai*— "house drying." Rice is put into attics for drying.
13. *gǫlę-yaloŋ-loŋ*— "the child cold month." The evenings are slightly cool but not as extreme as the following month.

Thus, timbral definitions of time rhythms hold for the broader level of months as well as for specific musical patterns.

For many Africans the year revolves around certain festivals and musical event occasions. Among the Talansi of northern Ghana, Cardinall observed that one year the Gologu festival occurred on March 1 and the next year it was observed on March 13, indicating that a quantitative numeration was not the primary way of scheduling the festival (1924:61-63). Some events are associated with the passage of the seasons and of the year. Among the Kabyle of Algeria the women go to the stables at winter solstice and make a great sound by beating metal pots and pans to awaken the cattle at the time that nature awakens (Bordieu 1963:57). Among peoples where Islam is important the feast at the end of Ramadan (Id Al-Fitir) and the pilgrimage to Mecca (Id Al-Hadha) are scheduled according to the Islamic lunar calendar.[48]

After harvest and during the lull in work, celebration and performance abound in the Kpelle area. The plentiful food supply, ready cash for new clothes and entertainment, and coincidence with the Western Christmas holidays all converge to make that time of the year one of general high spirits. Kulung could count on people wanting to spend time hearing the Wọi epic in this season. This is also the period when the closing of the Poro and Sande secret societies take place, for parents can afford to reclothe and feast their returned children with a ready surplus from harvest. Certainly the performance of Wọi epic is more frequent in this period. In short, the time following harvest is a time for increased social intercourse at an intensity that is not normal at other times of the year. Thus, music performance for the Kpelle follows definite yearly cycles and is much more frequent following the harvest and much less frequent at other times, particularly high work times. The same is true for many other African peoples who rely on the land for food, either as crops or as grass for grazing cattle.

The heavy work times are not devoid of music sound, however, for music often accompanies work, though Africans may not classify such work music with other music. The Birifor shepherd boys of Ghana make wind instruments of millet stalks and play musical signals for distant fellow shepherds, particularly as they move out to the fields in the morning (Nketia 1974:23). Among the Kpelle, slit-drum ensembles accompany the cooperative work crews clearing the thick forest growth. It is significant that Kulung recalls this work in several key phrases of his performance, using it as a metaphor for the precision that the ensemble must achieve.

The women planting rice may work to the music of slit drums or to their own unaccompanied call-response singing. When the rice is sown, and later, when it is ripening, young boys who guard the fields from the menacing flocks

48. See Fremont Besmer's linguistic structural analysis of one of these festivals (1974).

of weaver birds play the xylophone to fill the long, lonely hours. Even harvest brings group call-and-response singing, often filled with lewd and bawdy lyrics.

The reversal of given rules in the context of performance also characterizes the music event in Ghana.

> According to the traditions of the Brong area, the singing of songs of disparagement forms part of the worship of the god Ntoa, who has ordained that once a year, at a special festival lasting a whole week, his worshipers should get rid of all the ill feeling that they have been harboring during the year in song. It is, therefore, a time for group expression of public opinion in song and dance, a time for open criticism of those in authority, and for insulting individuals who may have misbehaved or offended others. . . . Any individual who has something to say must do so within a performing group by taking the solo lead or by getting the group to take up what he wants to express. (Nketia 1974:224)

RITUAL AND TIME IN LOCAL LIFE

Edmund Leach, following Durkheim, sets up a pattern which, he maintains, characterizes the time reckoning of many peoples. The key to the pattern is alternation between the sacred and the profane or the ritual and the nonritual. The sacred times are those of festivals, of rites that regularly recur in people's lives. They are often characterized by role changes where the identities of everyday lives become transformed during the ritual. Furthermore, in the sacred, time is often a reversal of the everyday profane onward flow (Leach 1961:134-36).

Though some researchers have confirmed Leach's pattern in African ritual, such findings need to be supported by more basic research into time concepts. The distinction Leach makes is an important one for social time, for ritual does seem to be a conceptual category that contrasts to nonritual. My own research among the Kpelle supports this premise. People create a distinctive local time when ritual is central to behavior and interaction.

Kpelle ritual events emphasize continuity and repetition. Cut-off cues are omitted. Nonritual time emphasizes segmentation, variation, and creativity. These are distinctions that are both recognized and verbalized. In the case of the wǫi-mẹni-pele the performance demonstrates aspects of both ritual and nonritual in a complex interweaving of the two. Nonritual segmentation is evident in the multi-ostinati sung by the chorus. Rather than respond in unison, the chorus performs in interlocking patterns, representing a fragmenting of sound. The storyteller employs considerable creative variation as he narrates each episode, drawing on the momentary ambience and atmosphere to inspire his directions. On the other hand, the episode units are obscured as the storyteller intermingles themes and characters of episodes. An upcoming episode is clearly foreshadowed before a present episode is concluded. Furthermore, continuity is demonstrated in that the storyteller never sings all the episodes he knows, so that his repertoire will appear to be infinite.

Maurice Bloch has gone to the extreme of suggesting that the nonlinear time reckoning perceived among various cultures by researchers is, in fact, ritual time. Scholars have failed, he maintains, to consider the time reckoning of ordinary profane time (1977:278-92). M. F. C. Bourdillon, in his critique of Bloch's article, counters that nondurational concepts of time do occur in everyday situations and are not confined to ritual occasions (1979:592).

The research on the Kpelle suggests that the notions of ritual and nonritual may be intermingled in a single interaction situation. One cannot neatly isolate each as Leach suggests (1961). Furthermore, the study of everyday time implies that linear time reckoning is not paramount in this area either. The entire scope of Kpelle time reckoning stresses factors other than durational concepts. Everyday time reckoning emphasizes the qualitative mosaic and differs from ritual time in significant ways.

LOCAL PRESENT, PAST, AND FUTURE

Time in African local life exhibits distinctive characteristics even in areas where urbanization and Western influence have introduced alternative modes of time reckoning. A key idea appears to be a focus on control of the present. People act to create in the present moment. Dale Eickelman notes of the Moroccans that "certain of their key temporal concepts, especially those concerning the present are shared with urban Moroccans" (1977:41). Furthermore, an art of passing time is evident, a measured creation of leisure. Among the Kabyle of Algeria, at leaving one says, "You are leaving us and we have hardly sat down and we have not spoken of everything" (Bordieu 1963:58). For the Kpelle, the present takes precedence to the extent that people tenaciously seek to fulfill interaction requirements of a situation in which they presently find themselves. They create the most of what is before them.

The past has been portrayed by some researchers as a static concept in African cultures. Warren d'Azevedo, however, maintains that for the Gola of Liberia the past constitutes an active mode of conception.

> The Gola approach to the past is dynamic rather than static. Its motives are highly instrumental and the past is regarded as a reservoir of negotiable property. (1962:33)

Robert Thornton also shows that the past for the Iraqw of Tanzania, as evidenced in lineage and clan, is expressed by spatial rather than chronological differentiation (1980:177). The past, for many peoples, is the authority by which actions are ordered in the present.

While many African peoples center activity in the present and look to a manipulable past to order that present, the future is not a mode of focus, as it is in many Western societies. For the Kuranko of Sierra Leone, the future lies outside of what constitutes time (Jackson 1977a:18). The Kabyle scoff at the idea of a vast and open future. They say, "The French act as if they would never die" (Bordieu 1963:55). When the future is of concern, divination often becomes an act that helps determine what course of action should be chosen in the present. This is the action in Wọi epic right before Wọi's wife gives birth. The anteater diviner is called to predict the future. As Thornton notes of the Iraqw of Tanzania, "Prophecy as a verbal performance links the present with the future, by implication, since what is seen must exist *in potentia* at the moment of the act of prophecy" (1980:177).

The everyday life as well as the special occasion of many African peoples is influenced by the social interaction within that society. To a considerable degree, activities and their recurrence serve to characterize the quality of time in which people live. Though clock time reckoning is possible and used to some extent, the social interaction appears, in many cases, to be fundamental in the ordering of life. The actions of the living are the focus of the present, while the acts of the ancestors and the acts of spirits influence the past and future respectively. Social acts thus become fundamental to the ordering of music events, and the very fabric of music making is bound up with the quality of social interaction. Cycles of recurring music events exist and are re-created year after year. But their occurrence is reckoned more by the quality of interaction than by durational measuring devices. And the Wọi epic reverberates these emphases with the front staging of social situations and the avoidance of any indication of quantitative time reckoning.

CHAPTER 8

Our Old People, Their Old People: The Epic and the Past

The time is now.

Taxi Motto

Time present and time past
Are both perhaps present in time future,
And time future contained in time past.

T. S. Eliot
"Burnt Norton"

The Wọi epic, for the Kpelle people, is one performance of their tradition. It is a description of their past, not in detailed terms, but in bold brushstrokes. As such, it describes the spirit and symbolic facts of their heritage as built by the interpretations of individual pourers. The hero represents an ancestor to whom they are all related. Some people say that they can point to the exact spot where Wọi disappeared into the ground when he left earth.

The Wọi epic presents both visibly and invisibly the Kpelle notion of the past and provides ways of re-creating that past in the present. In the largest sense, the Kpelle say that the Wọi epic tells about the origin of things and their beginnings. Thus Wọi's wife gives birth to all living things. The actions of Wọi's family illustrate the origins of things like jealousy, as captured in the episode of the jealous wife who must carve bowls with her voice. These episodes are exemplars of early Kpelle behavior for people to contemplate.

The epic is narrated predominantly in the present tense. The pourer brings the audience to a present-centered moment and involves them in what he performs as ongoing action.

Episode 1

One man called Ɣele-lawọ has caught one of Wọi's bulls and raised it behind the sky. And when you are going to Ɣele-

> lawọ's place, Squirrel-Monkey must climb in the dry tree quietly and get down behind the sky.

When past tense is used, it describes the immediate past of the present action:

> Wọi climbed, Wọi climbed. . .

This is followed by a move to the present:

> Wọi has arrived behind the sky, the bull has gotten down. The bull is really tall, the bees were on its horns.

Though there is a momentary—and entirely expected, in Kpelle terms—switch to the past in describing the bees, nothing is said to establish a year, a season, or the passage of time. We are shown one present-centered moment of battle or preparation for battle after another throughout the epic.

The singer does show subtle time passage in his song. This time passage occurs not within the story but within the development of the event. The narrative is unaffected by the passage of time. Rather, we are informed about time passage in relation to the performer and his building of the performance. Early in Episode One he uses the phrase "Sun-falling" to indicate time passing, and he repeats it in Episode Three. In Episode Six the phrase becomes "Sun-falling Maa-laa-ke-ma, it's the fight going there," and a few lines later, "Sun-falling, sun that doesn't wait until noon." Metaphorically Kulung is referring not so much to the story plot but to the quality of performance. As he compares the performance to the fight, he is indicating his satisfaction with the smooth playing and singing of the group. When shortly thereafter he mentions the "sun that doesn't wait until noon" he is alluding to his impatience at the audience coming forward with a small gift or, in the case of Kulung's preference, a drink. In Episode Eight his plea becomes more elaborate but no more direct. Here he sings, "Sun-falling, they are calling us again at night." By this he implies that he has by now sung not only a day's worth of work but a night's as well.

The passage of time is shown in order to depict a quality of feeling of the singer about his need to be rewarded. As the performance proceeds, his allusions are more developed and more poignant. This does not affect the telling of the story in the present-centered moment. The story is separated and compartmentalized from that flow of time.

Warren d'Azevedo, in stressing the manipulation of the past in the present in Gola historical accounts, notes the way that historical accounts are adjusted to suit present needs. A slight variation of this pattern comes in the Wọi epic. Here, elements of modern life are inserted into the old epic. For example, in another performance Kulung narrates an episode about Wọi's airplane moving into battle. Kulung reminds the audience that the airplane moved just like those do at Robert's Field, Liberia's international airport. The sounds to depict the moving of the plane curiously are exactly the same as the moving of the house. Thus the airplane substitutes for the house and the quality of motion is the same.

Certain details of the epic depict the old ways of doing things, however, and point to earlier times. The blacksmith is going to forge a needle to sew the war clothes. No mention is made of a sewing machine. Episode Eight mentions an iron bow and arrow rather than a gun.

THE PAST IN FORMAL RETROSPECT

The past, or history, as the concern of those engaged in formal retrospect is important to the Kpelle and many other African peoples who possess oral rather than written histories (d'Azevedo 1962). Historical time has been considered by historians to be, by and large, an objective and chronological time. In this sense, it is clocklike time writ large. John R. Hall critiques such an approach and analyzes the work of historians who have attempted to escape this approach (1980). While Fernand Braudel has differentiated historical time—identifying ephemeral moments, trends (social history), gradual change (structural history), and ecological history—he still maintains that all are united into one objective time (1972:20, 27). Louis Althusser and Etienne Balibar (1970), in Hall's view, adopt a Marxist structuralist approach whereby different levels of social formation have different times and do not conform to a single flux. Althusser, however, does not center on human subjects as actors or account for subjective time, a failing that Hall sees in the work of historians in general (Hall 1980:123-25).

History's avoidance of the subjective or inner time is not an altogether unnatural one, for the broad scope of time encompassed leads quite easily to such a situation. Furthermore, many historians maintain that they do take the subjective into account though their conclusions must necessarily be concerned with the broader perspective of events. The crux of the situation stems from lack of a clear indication of how the time experienced by individuals becomes the broad sweep of history. From the present perspective, a subjective experience by individuals must be a prerequisite to the broader interpretations of history. Historical trends live through the actions of people acting alone or together to create a society. Every characterization of style or epoch must ultimately be related back to that individual experience. Otherwise, historical time becomes a study of structures devoid of the human initiators.

The regard for an objective time, that not interpreted and shaped by man, seems to be part of musicologist-philosopher Charles Seeger's thinking when he says, "General space-time is for us, a given thing. Music space-time is man made" (1951:243). In such a view, time writ large does not become subject to man's shaping. And yet when we see how different are people's notions of past, present, and future, we must acknowledge clear differences at all levels of specificity. Historical time seems just as susceptible to shaping by man's interpretation as time within a song or the Wọi epic. Indeed for the Kpelle the epic of Wọi is part of their history and its recitation provides the spirit if not details of Kpelle culture.

THE KPELLE AND THE PAST

For the Kpelle in general and their construction of the Wọi epic in specific terms, cultural evolutionism, one of the ways that Western scholars have characterized historical time in Africa, has little resonance. Here are a people, after all, who stress continuity and eternity. They do not in the large historical picture view the world as evolving to ever higher and more complex forms. Indeed they do not focus much on a distant past, nor do they recite long genealogies of ancestors as do some other African peoples. Their world, even when contemplating the past, is present-centered. Though ideally that past is unchanged and unchanging, creative figuration of that past is in fact the order of the day, as in the insertion of the airplane motif in one version of the Wọi epic.

ORAL TRADITIONS

Our desire to know about the historical style of music like the Wọi epic is stifled in the view of a number of scholars by the lack of a written notation for music sound. This is seen as such a deficiency by Manfred Bukhofzer that he declares that "a historical study of the styles of non-Western music is at present an unattainable goal" because it "defies the traditional Western forms of notation and lacks the kind of historical documents we are accustomed to in our normal research" (1956:34). Fortunately, some scholars have persisted in the study of the history of music in Africa, and several perspectives are apparent today.

While some argue that the study of historical time is limited by lack of written documentation, others stress that much valuable information lies in oral traditions and that the ethnomusicologist can capitalize on this evidence. A fascinating example of the reproduction of oral history is the Kangaba ceremony held once every seven years where participants rebuild the *kama blo*, a building first raised by a descendant of Soundiata in Mali. One part of the performance includes a recitation of the Mande creation myth, "the story of the mythical generations" and "the genealogies of the Keita and of their related and allied lineages" (Dieterlen 1957:124).

As historian Jan Vansina has noted, the interpretation of oral tradition requires careful knowledge of the context so that manipulations that may occur may be understood (1965). Such caution, however, might well be made concerning the use of written histories as well, since "facts" recorded there have been selected to present particular viewpoints such as a history of great men or of the elite.

J. H. Kwabena Nketia comments on the value of oral history in the case of the xylophone among peoples of Ghana, where this instrument is integral to the history of the people and their migrations to the extent that groups are related according to, among other things, xylophone tunings and music (Nketia 1971:10; see also Goody 1956:7-16). In the state of Dahomey a centralized version of the oral history is available and this indicates that, dating back to the late 1600s, various kings were crucial to the development of innovative types of music and instrumental groupings (da Cruz 1954).

Nevertheless, given the importance of oral knowledge in African societies in general, even peoples who have not been part of a centralized state pass knowledge down from one elder to another. Among the people of Gbeyilataa in the Kpelle area of Liberia, for example, oral tradition explained that the harp-lute had been brought from the north and played in the area even though it was nowhere in evidence when I first began research in 1970. As an old drummer recounted to me,

> The [harp-lute player] came from Kpelle [the north] and they sold him. . . . He was a slave. They called him Harp-Lute-Player. He played the harp-lute for [the town founder]. A harp-lute they build on a large gourd. They stretched the string thus, they stretched the string thus, they stretched the string thus. . . . If they are playing it on that hill, if you can dance you will be here and dancing some. . . . Yes, when Gbeyila's heart was sweet, he danced. He had a large knife, larger than this and when he danced he took it out of the holder, he threw it in the air, and caught it. (Stone 1975:188-89)

He also described leg bells, which are no longer worn.

> These leg bells, our fathers wore them. It was Gọpu-zua and people like him who wore them. And Doo-kolo-gbayaŋ. These bells, a chief became rich, four or five of his wives wore them on their legs. When they are going to a town . . . the chief is behind them. All these women have bells on their legs. They go with them here. One of the people wearing bells, is in Massaquoitaa and they call her Gọọma. . . . The cheeks [of the bells] are seated like *weleŋ* [smaller bells]. . . . They come from Kpelle way like those little [bells]. That's the way it is but these are on iron. They attach them to iron. (Stone 1975:193-94)

A kind of oral tradition exists in song texts, which may be much more explicit about specific events than the Wọi epic. Peter Cooke and Martin Doornbos document texts that belong to protest songs of the Rwenzururu movement of the Bakonzo and Baamba people in western Uganda.

> This is the third tribal war in which many people are killed.
>
> The first one was Nyamutswa's. The second war was Kabalega's.
>
> A long time ago, we had Nyamutswa and Tibamwenda who refused to pay the tax graded by the Batoro. Then the Batoro killed them and buried them in one grave. (Cooke and Doornbos 1982:39)

Such evidence may also be presented in bits and pieces amidst a kaleidoscopic text. Musicians, whether in the factual or allusive texts, often give valuable hints about the past history of a people.

CHANGE AND THE LONG VIEW

Much of the early work with Western evolutionary and diffusionist models was derived from a few pieces of evidence fitted into a pattern. Later studies of change have been more restrictive in their conclusions and based on more extensive evidence. Nevertheless, seldom can researchers observe or experience the changes about which they write. Often a fieldworker conducts a study and then departs to write up conclusions. Ten or fifteen years later she returns to make another study. With the two studies in hand she then constructs a theory of what the processes are presumed to have been. She is like a photographer who takes two snapshots with an interval of time in between. She then attempts to surmise that happened between the two frozen portraits. Though she can describe a certain number of possibilities, she must remember that she did not actually experience that change. She did, in the latter instance, experience the end result.

Though some scholars have implied that little change has occurred in African music, more recent scholarship shows us that change has always occurred in the historical dimension. Certainly the evidence from oral history that da Cruz cites shows that Fon kings must have delighted in sponsoring new types of music during their reign. King Tegbouesson, who ruled from 1732 to 1775, presided over the introduction of the *agbaja, hanhye, gokoe,* and *gbolo* orchestras (1954). Certainly change is prevalent in present-day African societies, sometimes change of extreme dimensions. When I think of the Gbeyilataa group that I have studied over the last fifteen years during periodic visits, I can document precise aspects of the process. During fourteen months of fieldwork in 1975-76, I was able to observe perceptible changes from my first visit in 1970 that carry important implications for the people of that area. More important, by being fortunate enough to be a participant-observer of change during the field stay, I could use what Frederick Barth calls primary material rather than the deduction and extrapolation that is necessary in the "snapshot" considerations of change (Barth 1967:661-69).

A short time before I arrived, a young male singer and a supporting drummer came to the town. The singer brought with him a song, "Kọli-goŋ-soŋ," concerning the chief of the witches. During the fourteen months I observed, this song became the focal point for considerable activity. A dance was devised to accompany the song. Various wood formations were gathered in the forest to represent implements of the chief of the witches. Finally, an association was formed to support the performance of this music. Members included not only residents of Gbeyilataa but also migrants who worked in wage labor in rubber camps and in the capital city, Monrovia. These itinerants returned at month's end with money and ideas that served to shape this performance. The performance evolved before our eyes in a manner in which the people were both involved and aware of their involvement. They recognized that they were over the year developing a new performance association. The final act I observed in 1976 was the acquisition of white T-shirts to be worn by members of the group as a uniform. In the left-front corner of each was a heart with a number designation indicating rank within the group.

Change was evident in the introduction of a new performance style and group. The dance movements were strikingly different from those of the traditional dance. Movement was more continuous and less start-and-stop than is so characteristic of Kpelle dances. Yet the concept of the chief of the witches and the lack of cut-off cues, which indicate ritual elements, provided strong traditional currents and continuity to past practice. The song was interesting in that the solo/chorus responsory sections were longer than those in traditional performances and the interlock between the two was not as tight. The total effect was that of strong symbols of tradition bound up with fairly radical elements that represented change in Kpelle performance. To see these manipulated from performance to performance was exciting. Most characteristic was the change through accretion. The performers indicated that they thought about the cumulative effect of their actions. They conceived a gradual building up of the performance. As one player commented,

> Naatii is kọli-goŋ-soŋ's number two. He is the one who brought this song's way of dancing. When Kpanaa-loŋ arose with this song in Nọa-taa, he brought it to our place. We were performing one night. The second or third night, at that time they seated the Sande matter.[49] So the time they formed, they said we like it. We like this song. We can do it as a dancing thing, that which we can dance with outside. Let us buy things for it.
>
> And so Naatii was dancing and seating the inside of his feet. He was passing and taking those things [accoutrements] and imitating them variously. He said to them, "That song, that is the way to dance it because that is the song of a witch. And our witches are supposed to walk with their feet, the inside seated thus. Yes, Naatii brought that song's way of dancing." (Stone 1975:413)

Change is the result of individuals taking action, according to John Blacking, and should not be assumed to occur automatically: "Musical change is brought about by decisions made by individuals about music-making and music on the basis of their experiences of music in different social contexts" (Blacking 1977:14). Change is not *caused*, he goes on to say, by "contact among peoples and cultures" or "movement of populations" (see Nettl 1964:232). Blacking also cautions against using changes in society to explain music without examining the music. He also distinguishes between "innovation within a musical system" and "changes of the system." Such judgments should be made only within the context of social interaction (1977:19).

---

49. The time for the opening of the women's secret society session had been arranged. Poro sessions for the men alternate with Sande sessions for the women.

The results of extensive interchange among peoples in Africa is illustrated in Lester Monts's study of the song repertoire of the Vai people in Liberia and Roderic Knight's study of Manding songs. Instead of finding a body of "Vai" songs, Monts discovered that the Vai people performed Mende war songs, Islamic religious music of the Mandingo, and secret society songs of the Mende, Gola, and Dei (1981). Thus competence to handle this repertoire required knowledge of a number of neighboring societies and languages. Knight found considerable attention to Manding/Fula relations in the song texts of the Manding griots. These two peoples have lived in close contact in West Africa for a long period. As the griot sings in one song, "The Fula lunches on beef, he dines on beef, wealthy Fula" (Knight 1982:44).

A very prevalent kind of change in African music is the adoption of new sound-producing instruments to produce traditional music. David Rycroft cites the case of the Zulu replacing the music bow and gourd resonator with a guitar to play their indigenous music (1977:245). Klaus P. Wachsmann cites a similar case in Uganda: "In the case of the fiddle, the stimulus for its invention and the impetus for its astonishing social career came from foreign sources, but its music was nevertheless indigenous . . ." (1958:54-55). For the Kpelle in Liberia, a beer bottle tapped with the back edge of a penknife has replaced the boat-shaped iron idiophone, a change that has not appreciably altered the timbre produced, despite the radical difference in form.

The changes that occur in African music often relate to influences from other dominant cultures. People choose particular ways of responding to them. The Yoruba response to the influence of Islam is a fascinating example. In this case, Muslim musicians participate in the worship of indigenous gods. Indeed, Akin Euba credits Yoruba Muslims with keeping Yoruba music alive. In this instance, traditional Yoruba music, rather than Islamic music, is used in religious Muslim festivals (1971). A number of African instruments have evolved from Arabic examples, and Aning shows evidence for the development of the Akan atumpan drum from the Arabic tabl (1977).

Certainly influences from Western civilization have had an impact on African musics. In some areas where this has led to a denigration and devaluing of local tradition for a time, a later interest in traditional forms has resurged. A conspicuous example is the revival of traditional dance forms with choreography for stage presentation and the creation of national dance troupes in a number of African countries. These groups are employed to instill national pride and to symbolize national unity to the outside world (Hanna 1973:167).

Contrary to the view of some that African societies in general and African musics in particular do not change, some scholars have perceived a more dynamic approach to the past on the part of Africans. Warren d'Azevedo is one such person. He has documented how the Gola use the past in an active way, adjusting it for their instrumental purposes (1962). In such a setting, a comprehensive history is discouraged. Great variation exists depending upon a private or public rendering. When consensus is reached, compromise of a number of versions is the result (1962:18-19). And although the ancestors continue to concern themselves with human affairs, the Gola do not stress chronology in relating genealogies.

> In this context, information concerning chronological sequence in depth or the correlation of parallel genealogic sequences is considered irrelevant and is seldom volunteered. It is the quality of an event or a cluster of events, which is the focus of interest. (d'Azevedo 1962:28)

Thus the stress on the qualitative for historical time is remarkably similar to that placed on other dimensions of African time.

Gilbert Rouget's analysis of court songs in Dahomey very nicely illustrates d'Azevedo's assertions. In Porto-Novo the songs at court are not sung so much to reiterate and preserve facts unaltered as they are to actively reconstruct the past. Allusiveness and ambiguity are strong features designed to present obscure meanings of these songs of praise and insult. While the first stanza is addressed to the present king, the subsequent verses, which are addressed to past kings, vary in the kings included (1971:35).

A major concern in looking at historical time in Africa is whether ethnomusicologists can legitimately derive an objective meaning from facts and items they find or whether it is crucial to know something of the meanings attached to those elements by the people who created them. This concern recapitulates the argument made by Hall regarding subjective time and objective time. Merriam, in an essay published posthumously, argues that ethnomusicologists should and must compare forms without necessarily accounting for meaning, when he criticizes "the rejection of the utility of one kind of comparison—the comparison of forms—and an emphasis on the priority of another kind of comparison—that of meanings" (1982:175).

When Merriam argues for such a comparison he implies, it seems to me, that form can be examined devoid of and apart from meaning. I would counter that all form has at least syntactic meaning. The question is whether the meaning has been supplied by the people who created it and inferred by the researcher, or simply supplied by the researcher. Merriam, it appears, is arguing for study of form with the meaning supplied by the researcher. Merriam's position is quite different from that of John Blacking, who, in his discussion of historical time, says, "If musical evidence is to be used in reconstructing African history, musical styles must be carefully described both as patterns of social and cultural action and as patterns of sound" (1971:186). Blacking illustrates his position with an example from the Venda.

> It is only when one talks with Venda about the sociological background to musical performances that they begin to reveal the diversity which underlies this apparent homogeneity: subtle differences in musical style express both the cleavages and alignments in Venda society, and hence the social significance of the music and its impact on different individuals, and some of the historical origins of those divisions. (1971:190)

Many are familiar with the common practice of classifying musical styles on the basis of the frequency of various ascending and descending intervals. Blacking points out that to do so for the Venda would not reveal that apparently different melodies are regarded as one and the same through the principle of "harmonic equivalence" (1971:191).

The web of historical temporality is, as we have attempted to show here, a multilayered one. The unilinear evolution and diffusion plans that proceed with clocklike regularity do not adequately provide a realistic picture of change in the musical context where Wọi epic is performed. Change in historical time for the Kpelle people who create the Wọi epic, for some other Africans, and for some historians, proceeds in a dynamic fashion that surges and pauses at various levels of the whole at any one moment. The past is dynamic and not fixed in nature. It is subject to manipulation within the present context of action. It is thus doubly imperative that our theoretical orientations allow for such flexibility.

The need is to observe, where possible, actual forces of change and document them. We require firsthand observations of ebb and flow of historical time in music, even in the short run, to grasp even remotely what some rhythms of historical time might be. Our steps of inference are too numbered to understand historical time well. We need to know more of the ways that people like the Kpelle have of understanding the past through media such as the Wọi epic.

CHAPTER 9

Epic and Time in Perspective

. . . at the still turning point, there the dance is.
T. S. Eliot
"Burnt Norton"

Time exists only as a participant, a performer or an audience member, experiences it. Time flux is partially shared by people who make music together and, to the extent that it is shared, a vital synchrony results. Their interpretation of that time must be regarded in seeking to understand it.

The coordination of time dimensions in Kpelle and, I think, other African music provides a kind of "essential tension."[50] This is represented very concretely by the soloist and supporting singer (tomo-soŋ-nuu) relationship in Kpelle performance, for here the soloist creates and weaves proverbs and allusory texts in a composition of split-second timing that fits with the regularly recurring supporting singer pattern. As the performers and listeners alike are moved to inner time dimensions by this artistry, they are aware, if only peripherally, of the supporting singer, who sings a never varying *ostinato* that alternates with the soloist's fanciful variations. The supporting singer is moving in outer time, maintaining that dimension in an essential tension with the soloist's movements toward inner time.

The Wọi epic is a microcosm of these multiple dimensions. The speech and music that organize the performers and keep them on track move in a kind of outer time. Here the nuts and bolts of keeping things together takes place. Discussions of raising a song in the small voice rather than the large voice and placing a part properly are all standard. Midway between outer and inner time the narrative of the story is spoken, often in heightened speech, in colorful and rhythmic language. The audience is moved to another world, much of that world emphasizing the mechanics of action. The house moves, the squirrel climbs, the bird pumps the bellows. The song of the epic pourer is where, in allusive phrases and deep proverbs, the really emotionally vivid life appears.

50. This term has been used by Thomas Kuhn for the relationship between convergent thinkers and divergent thinkers in the sciences (1977:225-39).

Through music and through the words of music, a special kind of experience is possible, prepared by the movement through the background layers of outer time. Of special interest is the rapid movement from outer to inner time and back again as the epic unfolds.

Another kind of essential tension exists between the qualities of ritual activity and those of nonritual activity. Nonritual music, with its constant change, segments, and layering, is quite different from the ritual, which continues endlessly, monolithic and unchanged. In the epic these elements exist simultaneously. The continuity between episodes reflects the ritual aspect while the creative segmentation of the mosaiclike bits and pieces reflects the nonritual aspect. An incredibly tight balance appears between the two themes, the eternal versus the segment, sometimes showing one in dominance, sometimes showing the other. The uniqueness of Kpelle epic time, and, indeed, of time in Kpelle aesthetic expression, rests on the stress given the qualitative elements. While the elements in themselves are not unique, the way they are emphasized particularly through movement and layering is distinctive. The nuance of placement provides a subtle and yet striking approach to organizing music.

As we consider musical expression, viewed from each of the time perspectives, it becomes apparent that the Kpelle, and perhaps other Africans, favor qualitative aspects, eschewing the quantitative and, therefore, linear perspective. Whether timbral nuances are used to coordinate rhythm, or spatial differentiations to communicate time, qualitative distinctions prevail, even in the outer dimension.

The qualitative/quantitative aspects of time can be separated into distinct levels of analysis. First, we can begin with the most specific and fine-grained element—that of the song. Here we find the kind of time that is referred to as musical rhythm, a level where many of us settle our attention. Song time for the Kpelle is dominated by qualitative elements of timbre, segmentation, and variation juxtaposed against constancy.

A more encompassing level is that of event time, a musical event incorporating a whole evening of songs, laughter, speech, and perhaps feasting. Events, like songs, have many qualitative aspects to their time. Beginnings in both are drawn out and endings often abrupt. The quality of performance and total group interaction determines much about the length of time an event continues. The epic as one kind of event shows the ritual overlay of continuity and seamlessness onto the segmentation and variation.

Another time flow is that of biographical time. Each participant in epic has an individual trajectory from birth to death and, perhaps, to ancestorhood. For the Kpelle an individual's life proceeds not so much in quantitative terms, though the Kpelle do certainly recognize the passing of time or the aging process. Rather, childhood can last an elastic number of years depending on the point of initiation into the Poro or Sande, which marks movement to adulthood. Also, movement to old age confers high status on people, and particularly increases access to knowledge.

Interrelated to biographical time is the life cycle, which for the Kpelle consists of certain life crisis rites or events. These are heavily regulated by ritual, and this time flow, more than any of the others, emphasizes the quantitative.

The time flow of everyday life, which we might refer to as social time, moves as the interaction of people proceeds. For the Kpelle this time is qualitative, built on continuing transaction to maintain its flux.

Calendar time as the Kpelle conceive it is not reckoned with careful precision in quantitative terms, except when the Kpelle shift to using the Western Gregorian calendar. Yet the qualities of the days and, more important, of the seasons are noticed. The weekly rotating market days are a recent addition in most areas, brought by a network of roads and a demand for produce in the urban areas.

Historical time, that flow of time which proceeds in the broadest perspective, is very important qualitatively to the Kpelle. It provides authority for the present action. But it is not of great depth, nor is it figured linearly or quantitatively. Rather, it is continually adjusted to suit the needs of the present moment.

Perhaps the subtlety of these time flows is the reason they are so easy to miss. Perhaps this is why Western ethnomusicologists can apply other grids without great problem. The results can be viewed other ways if one disregards the perspective of those musicians who create the music and of the audience who responds to it.

To confuse things even further, with Western ideas being quickly infused into Kpelle and, perhaps, other performance in Africa, one does find examples of clocklike time where such time has been adopted.

In my own research, however, I have found that concepts suggested by the Kpelle data are often corroborated with examples from other African peoples. Indeed I have, along the way, referred to examples from North Africa that underscore points made about Kpelle ideas, and from my recent work in Arabia I find certain broad congruences as well. The sharp dividing line that has been implied in some of the literature between North Africa and sub-Saharan Africa is not nearly as clear as sometimes described. Isolated statements in the literature and some of my own fieldwork suggest parallels even with North Africa and Arabia.

If we accept that some peoples organize the outer time of their musics in a predominantly qualitative fashion, then the implications are pervasive, for we must accept some fundamentally different ways of approaching music.

The problem that must trouble us is how precision of coordination can exist in time reckoning that is not quantitative. With a clock as the symbol of Western time coordination, we question what coordination is possible in nonquantitative time. The careful timing in Kpelle and other African music, commonly acknowledged to require extreme precision, is surprising. If such precision of synchronization is possible, then is not coordination possible at a much higher level as well? Arguments against nonquantitative time-reckoning schemes have often centered on the fact that linear time is a prerequisite, but not the only one, for industrial, scientific development. Cyclical time, the characterization of African time, inhibits cooperation among large numbers of people, the kind of group effort necessary for industrial, scientific development. Since this study has concentrated on music, the conclusions can only be based on that part of human life. Nevertheless, the evidence from African music does not support the argument against large-scale cooperation. In the events studied, many people synchronize their activities in complex ways extending beyond what anyone should expect who makes the generalization regarding the superiority of linear time. If such precision is possible on a small scale, what makes it unexpected at a level where the precision required may not be as great? The fact that linear time is predominant in most cultures should not allow us to conclude that it represents the only possible mode of time reckoning that can lead to technological development.

As I have elsewhere emphasized, African music research has long looked at music at the level of song (Stone 1982). Thus music has been studied in Africa from an item perspective. There is little information concerning the historical styles of music in Africa, to say nothing of the lives of musicians, or even the social time reckoning. Furthermore, study has centered on the outer dimension of song. Little is known or commented upon concerning inner time, a most vital and dynamic aspect of music.

The future study of time in African music embraces a large area. Ideally, researchers will consider the various kinds of musical time within a single study even if they choose to focus on one particular kind. This will afford us data that integrate a variety of times rather than data that view time as unidimensional. Even more critical, we need to consider music as a process as well as a product or item, applying the perspective of the African peoples to the motion, the dynamism, that is the essence of music for so many societies. The results of such studies should provide us with a much richer and more detailed view of African performance. We presently see a mere part of a sketch.

Ethnomusicologists have good reasons to consider time more carefully. First, they possess professional training to consider rhythm at a microlevel. Rhythm at the level of song is something that has long been studied. Second, time provides important clues not only about the making of music but, no doubt, about the broader fabric of social life. While I would not maintain that the rhythms of music are determined by aspects of social life, they are certainly interrelated. Time in one domain of life links up and is related in some fashion to time in another domain. As a consequence, rhythm in music and in overall time organization is of interest to social and cultural anthropologists, folklorists, and historians, crosscutting the formerly rigid disciplinary boundaries that artificially divide the whole of African social life.

The critic may still protest that the nature of time in Kpelle epic is still not all that different from time in any other music. The answer must rest in the ultimate shape and configuration of that time which, though composed of the same elements as any other time, becomes specially fashioned. Much like the writing of Gabriel Okara, an Ijaw of Nigeria, who so ably renders in English the special flavor of Ijaw expression, Kpelle ideas of time are carefully shaped.

> Outside he walked strongly with no fear in his feet and no fear in his inside. But as he passed, women moved away from his front, casting bad eyes at him and from dark interiors of houses people looked at him with Chief Izongo's eyes and behind him walked his friends, walking with Chief Izongo's feet. (Okara 1964:41)

In the end, the differences are quite profound, and they change one's entire perspective. They show us how wispy the concepts we seek are, how fragile they seem as we move through data looking for the overwhelming and the powerful. Those who understand this artistry may be the ones who have overlooked it in searching for more overwhelming answers.

The future of ethnomusicology in general and of studies of African arts in particular is affected by these findings in a number of ways. First, study in African arts draws on a multidisciplinary base. Time as discussed here would customarily be studied by at least three separate disciplines. Yet in the context of African music performance these disciplines interlink quite closely. Within a single music performance, music, dance, and the plastic arts are parts of a conceptual whole that the Kpelle find difficult to separate. We need to avoid creating study objects that are artificial to Kpelle thinking.

Second, techniques and concepts for analysis of qualitative aspects need to be developed. With the Western bias for quantitative analysis, we possess very crude techniques for understanding things expressed in qualitative terms. It is striking that timbre, for example, an aspect so strongly emphasized in temporal delineation, is perhaps the least developed area of Western musical style analysis. We have only crude terminology for describing timbre, and, as scholars, little training in studying this area. Yet the data reveal how important this particular dimension becomes for understanding time where the Kpelle and other Africans are concerned.

Third, models need to reflect a capacity to study a number of analytic levels. The nature of academic disciplines is partially reflected by the tendency to use models that are not capable of encompassing several levels. One model can focus specifically at song but not broadly at large time intervals like history embraces. The difficulty in working with a number of models which focus at a number of levels is that they often project fundamentally different assumptions.

The Kpelle case, many might argue, is not unique. Certainly other peoples, including Westerners, stress qualitative or three-dimensional spatial characteristics. If we seek to judge the case by any single criterion, a great many different points can be made with the same data. What gives time in the Kpelle experience its special quality is the total configuration of all the time levels seen as a coordinated set. If we consider music in time, for example, and look at all the time levels included, we can begin to see what is involved.

Time, from a Kpelle perspective, for example, moves qualitatively for the most part. The fitting together of one part to another in outer song time is accomplished by resort to mnemonic devices based on verbal language. Musicians refer to how various parts fit and relate to one another, in many respects reflecting multiple points of organization. Though the struck idiophone provides an unvarying rhythmic pattern and can be one of the focal points, musicians are not single-mindedly relating to this one pattern. In the Kpelle case at least, it would be a mistake to think that there is a single beat or pattern that is the essential glue.

What is stronger evidence that the dominant time patterning in music is qualitative is the way that very intricate patterns are executed. Kpelle musicians, from the present evidence, do not rely on counting or numbering to conceptualize and properly execute their patterns. Verbal sounds and voice timbres indicate to them how a pattern will proceed.

Phases of the event are realized as the quality of social interaction indicates such change is appropriate. The Kpelle epic singer is rewarded for his efforts through excitement and tokens of praise. The biography of an individual certainly affects what happens in the musical event. For a Kpelle singer, the past provides important and essential references for the present performance. The life span becomes a reservoir that is a reference, though quantitative linear organization is not prominent. Linear progression appears crucial in the understanding of ideas about how a person is born, matures, and dies, though death is often viewed as simply a move to ancestor status rather than as a final disappearing unlike other life statuses.

Social action impinges on musical performance through its larger patterns. The quality of this interaction affects what happens to enable events to take place. This social time becomes a fundamental mode for ordering musical activities. Within this, the unit of the day, as a kind of present, is the focus for life and planning of activities. Within this present, a great elaboration of activity is both possible and frequent. It appears that this present can be embroidered to an extent that Westerners rarely experience.

History in the making of Kpelle music is most important but not fundamentally quantitative. The past becomes essential authorization for activity in the present. The past is also considered dynamic and active, changing within the present situation as people regard it in new light and context. Singers invite the participation of ancestors in events and recite historical events to validate a present course of action. The past is vital to the creation of music and it is a viable and dynamic element in that creation.

We see that the Kpelle do recognize quantitative aspects of time, particularly as part of ritual activities. These elements are of much less interest than are the qualitative and spatial dimensions. The qualitative elements are treated with the attention accorded to quantitative elements in Western time conceptualization. For this reason, the entire fabric of musical time exudes a different character.

In the past, the quantitative has been equated with precision and accuracy. Since Kpelle music shows that considerable precision is evident with predominantly qualitative reckoning, we now need to accept that the deemphasis of the quantitative does not mean the absence of precise time reckoning. Alternative modes of reckoning time create exciting new vistas for ethnomusicological study. Now we can broaden our approaches to time, enlarging our theoretical vocabulary as we study more systematically this exciting data from more cosmopolitan perspectives. We may, in the process, also find a liberation from the linear quantitative straitjacket that has guided much research.

Only through equal attention to theory and data will the clearer view of Kpelle musical time emerge. Only through concern for music as created and understood by the Kpelle and other Africans will we better grasp what is only now crudely sketched as time in the wọi-mẹni-pele.

GLOSSARY OF KPELLE NAMES AND TERMS

bẹlẹ — kind of tree which blocks the progress of Wọi's house.

fẹ̀li — goblet-shaped drum played with the hands by the master drummer.

gboto — a kind of frog; in chorus a group of them announce the passing of Wọi's house.

Gelengoi — Wọi's jealous wife, whom he banishes to the fork of the road to carve bowls with her voice.

Gemila — spirit that opposes Wọi and plucks out eyes when it fights.

gọọ — kind of frog; in chorus they respond to the gboto frogs, announcing the passing of Wọi's house.

Kelema-ninga — another name for the Tuu-tuu-Bird.

Koing — kind of tree which becomes an obstacle to the movement of Wọi's house.

koong — leaf from a tree that is used occasionally to thatch houses; aids Wọi by serving as a trap for Bat, who is assaulting Wọi's house.

Kpayang-miling — one of the names of Beetle, who is an ally of Wọi; also known as Kpokiling.

Kpokiling — one of the names of Beetle, who is an ally of Wọi; also known as Kpayang-miling.

Kulung — singer-storyteller of epic version included in text.

lele — a kind of small squirrel monkey.

Maa-laa-kẹ-ma — tutelary spirit that Kulung calls to enhance his rendition of the epic.

Maa-pu — Wọi's daughter, who helps Wọi fight his enemies, particularly to set fire to the bẹlẹ tree.

Malong-yaa-pu — another name for Wọi's jealous wife Gelengoi.

Mare-kẹẹ-kẹ-nuu — questioner, who prods storyteller-singer at appropriate moments in the epic.

Mẹni-maa-fa — a spirit that is an enemy of Wọi and manifests itself as a lizard at times.

mẹni-pele — chante-fable; dramatized folktale that is accompanied by instruments and a choral background.

muu — short repeating pattern sung by a part of the chorus.

nyii-pere — "sleep road"; dream.

pele — musical event; children's play; game.

Poling — beautiful bird who is an ally of Wọi the hero.

Poro — generic West African term for men's secret society to which all men belong. In Kpelle specifically, pọlọng.

Sande — generic West African term for women's secret society to which all women belong. In Kpelle specifically, saning.

tomo — repeating ostinato pattern sung between solo lines.

tomo-soŋ-nuu — "tomo-catching-person"; supporting singer.

Tuu-tuu — bird that pumps the bellows to help forge a needle to sew Wọi's war clothes.

wẹsẹ — sound of a millet stalk breaking; part of the formula for the ending of an epic episode. The storyteller-singer sings, "Ding kpala kẹ, wẹsẹ," and the chorus responds, "Wẹsẹ."

Wọi-boi — Wọi's younger son, who aids him in his battles.

wọi-mẹni-pele — epic that tells of the life and adventures of the hero Wọi; includes instrumental accompaniment and choral background.

wule — song.

ɣele-kọlọng — the near sky, which one can see and upon which one can sit.

Ɣele-lawọ — a spirit that is an enemy of Wọi and also manifests itself as a bitter rattan plant.

ɣele-polu — "behind the sky"; the distant sky, which exists beyond the near sky.

Zoo-lang-kee — spirit of a deceased performer that is called to the epic performance to enhance the quality of the event.

Zu-kpeei — Wọi's older son, who aids him in his battles.

REFERENCES CITED

Abimbola, Wande. 1971. "Stylistic Repetition in Ifá Divination Poetry." *Lagos Notes and Records* 3(1):38-53.

Abraham, R. C. 1940. *The Tiv People.* 2nd ed. London: Crown Agents.

Adams, Charles R. 1974. "Ethnography of Basotho Evaluative Expression in the Cognitive Domain *Lipapali* (Games)." Ph.D. dissertation, Indiana University.

Agar, Michael. 1980. "Stories, Background Knowledge and Themes: Problems in the Analysis of Life History Narrative." *American Ethnologist* 7(2):223-39.

Althusser, Louis, and Etienne Balibar. 1970. *Reading Capital.* 1968. Translated by Ben Brewster. London: NLB.

Ames, David W. 1973. "A Sociocultural View of Hausa Musical Activity." In *The Traditional Artist in African Societies,* edited by Warren L. d'Azevedo, pp. 128-61. Bloomington: Indiana University Press.

Aning, Ben. 1977. "Atumpan Drums: An Object of Historical and Anthropological Study." In *Essays for a Humanist: An Offering to Klaus Wachsmann,* pp. 58-71. New York: Town House Press.

Armstrong, Robert Plant. 1971. *The Affecting Presence.* Urbana: University of Illinois Press.

Babalola, S. A. 1964-65. "The Characteristic Features of Outer Form of Yoruba Ijala Chants." *Odu* 1(1):33-44, and (2):47-77.

Barth, Frederick. 1967. "On the Study of Social Change." *American Anthropologist* 69:661-69.

Barthold, Bonnie J. 1981. *Black Time: Fiction of Africa, the Caribbean, and the United States.* New Haven: Yale University Press.

Bartle, Philip F. 1978. "Forty Days: The Akan Calendar." *Africa* 48(1):80-84.

Bateson, Gregory. 1972. *Steps to an Ecology of the Mind.* New York: Ballantine.

Batuta, Ibn. 1858. *Voyages d'Ibn Batoutah.* Translated by C. Defrémery and B.R. Sanguinetti. Paris: Imprimerie Nationale.

Bauman, Richard. 1977. *Verbal Art as Performance.* Rowley, Mass.: Newbury House.

Bebey, Francis. 1975. *African Music: A People's Art.* Translated by Josephine Bennett. Westport: Lawrence Hill.

Becker, Alton L. 1979. "Text-Building, Epistemology, and Aesthetics in Javanese Shadow Theatre." In *The Imagination of Reality: Essays in Southeast Asian Coherence Systems,* edited by A. L. Becker and Aram A. Yengoyan, pp. 211-43. New Jersey: Ablex.

Beidelman, Thomas O. 1963. "Kaguru Time Reckoning: An Aspect of the Cosmology of an East African People." *Southwestern Journal of Anthropology* 19:9-20.

Ben-Amos, Dan. 1972. "Two Benin Storytellers." In *African Folklore,* edited by Richard M. Dorson, pp. 103-114. Garden City, New York: Anchor/Doubleday.

Berliner, Paul. 1978. *The Soul of Mbira.* Berkeley: University of California Press.

Besmer, Fremont E. 1974. *Kídàn dárán sállà: Music for the Eve of the Muslim Festivals 'Id Al-Fatir and 'Id Al-Kabir in Kano, Nigeria.* Bloomington: African Studies Program, Indiana University.

Biebuyck, Daniel, and Kahombo C. Mateene, eds. and trans. 1971. *The Mwindo Epic.* Berkeley: University of California Press.

Blacking, John. 1955. "Some Notes on a Theory of African Rhythm Advanced by Erich von Hornbostel." *African Music* 1(2):12-20.

______. 1969. *Process and Product in Human Society*. Johannesburg: Witwatersrand University Press.

______. 1971. "Music and the Historical Process in Vendaland." In *Essays on Music and History in Africa*, edited by Klaus P. Wachsmann, pp. 185-212. Evanston: Northwestern University Press.

______. 1973. *How Musical Is Man?* Seattle: University of Washington Press.

______. 1977. "Some Problems of Theory and Method in the Study of Musical Change." *Yearbook of the International Folk Music Council* 9:1-26.

Bledsoe, Caroline. 1980. *Women and Marriage in Kpelle Society*. Stanford: Stanford University Press.

Bloch, Maurice. 1977. "The Past and the Present in the Present." *Man* 12:278-82.

Bohannan, Paul. 1953. "Concepts of Time Among the Tiv of Nigeria." *Southwestern Journal of Anthropology* 9(3):251-62.

Bordieu, Pierre. 1963. "The Attitude of the Algerian Peasant Toward Time." In *Mediterranean Countrymen*, edited by J. Pitt-Rivers, pp. 55-72. The Hague: Mouton.

______. 1977. *Outline of a Theory of Practice*. Translated by Richard Nice. Cambridge: Cambridge University Press.

Bourdillon, M. F. C. 1979. "Knowing the World or Hiding It: A Response to Maurice Bloch." *Man* 13:591-9.

Boyd, Alan. 1977. "The Dimension of Time in the Definition of the Situation with Reference to *Maulidi*." Unpublished manuscript.

Brain, James L. 1973. "Ancestors as Elders in Africa—Further Thoughts." *Africa* 43(2):122-33.

Brandel, Rose. 1961. *The Music of Central Africa*. The Hague: Martinus Nijhoff.

Braudel, Fernand. 1972. *The Mediterranean and the Mediterranean World in the Age of Philip the Second*. 1966. Translated by Sian Reynolds. New York: Harper and Row.

Bril, Blandine. 1979. "Analyse des hombres associés à l'homme et à la femme en Afrique de l'Ouest." *Africa* 49(4):367-76.

Brink, James T. 1981. "Time Consciousness and Growing Up in Bamana Folk Drama." Paper presented at the Indiana University African Studies Program Seminar: African Dimensions of Time. Spring semester.

Bukhofzer, Manfred. 1956. "Observations on the Study of Non-Western Music." In *Colloques de Wégimont*, edited by Paul Collaer, pp. 33-36. Brussels: Elsevier.

Burton, John W. 1981. "'The Moon is a Sheep': A Feminine Principle in Atuot Cosmology." *Man* 16(3):441-50.

Busia, K. A. 1954. "The Ashanti." In *African Worlds: Studies in Cosmological Ideas and Social Values of African Peoples*, edited by Daryll Forde, pp. 190-209. London: Oxford University Press.

Cardinall, A. W. 1924. "The Division of the Year among the Talansi of the Gold Coast." *Man* 47:66-83.

Chernoff, John Miller. 1979. *African Rhythm and African Sensibility*. Chicago: University of Chicago Press.

Cooke, Peter, and Martin Doornbos. 1982. "Rwenzururu Protest Songs." *Africa* 52(1):37-60.

da Cruz, Clément. 1954. "Les Instruments de musique dans le Bas-Dahomey." *Etudes dahoméennes* 12:15-79.

Danquah, J. B. 1928. *Gold Coast: Akan Laws and Customs and the Akim Abuakwa Constitution*. London: Routledge.

d'Azevedo, Warren L. 1962. "Uses of the Past in Gola Discourse." *Journal of African History* 3(1):11-34.

______. 1973. "Sources of Gola Artistry." In *The Traditional Artist in African Societies*, pp. 282-340. Bloomington: Indiana University Press.

De Vale, Sue Carole. 1984. "Prolegomena to a Study of Harp and Voice Sounds in Uganda: A Graphic System for the Notation of Texture." In *Selected Reports in Ethnomusicology: Volume V, Studies in African Music*, edited by J. H. Kwabena Nketia and Jacqueline Cogdell Djedje, pp. 285-315. Los Angeles: University of California Program in Ethnomusicology.

Dieterlen, Germaine. 1941. *Les âmes des Dogons*. Paris: Travaux et Mémoires de l'Institut d'Ethnologie, vol. 40.

______. 1957. "The Mande Creation Myth." *Africa* 27:124-37.

Douglas, Mary. 1954. "The Lele of Kasai." In *African Worlds: Studies in the Cosmological Ideas and Social Values of African Peoples*, edited by Daryll Forde, pp. 1-26. London: Oxford University Press.

Dyson-Hudson, Neville. 1963. "The Karimojong Age System." *Ethnology* 2:353-401.

Eickelman, Dale F. 1977. "Time in a Complex Society: A Moroccan Example." *Ethnology* 16:39-55.

Eliot, T. S. 1971. *The Complete Poems and Plays 1909-1950*. New York: Harcourt, Brace and World.

Euba, Akin. 1971. "Islamic Musical Culture among the Yoruba: A Preliminary Survey." *Essays on Music and History in Africa*, edited by Klaus Wachsmann, pp. 171-81. Evanston: Northwestern University Press.

Evans-Pritchard, E. E. 1940. *The Nuer*. Oxford: Oxford University Press.

Faris, J. C. 1973. "'Occasions' and 'Non-Occasions.'" In *Rules and Meanings*, edited by Mary Douglas, pp. 45-59. Harmondsworth: Penguin.

Finnegan, Ruth. 1970. *Oral Literature in Africa*. London: Oxford University Press.

Friedman, Robert. 1982. "Making an Abstract World Concrete: Knowledge, Competence and Structural Dimensions of Performance among Batá Drummers in Santeria." Ph.D. dissertation, Indiana University.

Gay, John H., and Michael Cole. 1967. *The New Mathematics in an Old Culture; A Study of Learning Among the Kpelle of Liberia*. New York: Holt, Rinehart and Winston.

Geest, Sjaak van der. 1980. "The Image of Death in Akan Highlife Songs." *Research in African Literatures* 11(2):145-74.

Gennep, Arnold van. 1960. *The Rites of Passage*. 1909. Translated by M. B. Vizedom and G. L. Caffee. London: Routledge and Keagan Paul.

Gibbs, James L. 1965. "The Kpelle of Liberia." In *People of Africa*, pp. 197-240. New York: Holt, Rinehart and Winston.

Giddens, Anthony. 1979. *Central Problems in Social Theory: Action Structure and Contradiction in Social Analysis*. Berkeley: University of California Press.

Gidley, C. G. B. 1975. "*Roko*: A Hausa Praise Crier's Account of His Craft." *African Language Studies* 16:93-115.

Glaze, Anita. 1981. *Art and Death in a Senufo Village*. Bloomington: Indiana University Press.

Goldberg, Alan. 1980. "Art, Play, Ritual and Morality in Performance Events." Paper presented at the Meeting of the Society for Ethnomusicology, Bloomington, Indiana, November 21.

Goody, Jack. 1956. *The Social Organization of the Lowiili.* London: Her Majesty's Stationery Office.

Gourlay, Kenneth. 1972. "The Practice of Cueing Among the Karimojoŋ of North-East Uganda." *Ethnomusicology* 16:240-49.

Griaule, Marcel. 1948. *Dieu d'eau: Entretiens avec Ogotemmêli.* Paris: Editions du Chêne.

Gurvitch, Georges. 1964. *The Spectrum of Social Time.* Dordrecht: D. Riedel.

Hall, John R. 1980. "The Time of History and the History of Times." *History and Theory* 19(2):113-31.

Hamer, John H. 1970. "Sidamo Generational Class Cycles: A Political Gerontocracy." *Africa* 40(1):50-70.

Hanna, Judith Lynne. 1973. "African Dance: The Continuity of Change." *Yearbook of the International Music Council* 5:165-74.

Harries, Jeanette. 1973. "Pattern and Choice in Berber Weaving and Poetry." *Research in African Literatures* 4(2):141-63.

Horton, Robin. 1967. "African Traditional Thought and Western Science." *Africa* 37:50-71, 155-87.

Irvine, Judith T. 1978. "When is Genealogy History? Wolof Genealogies in Comparative Perspective." *American Ethnologist* 5(4):651-74.

Jackson, Michael. 1977a. *The Kuranko: Dimensions of Social Reality in a West African Society.* New York: St. Martin's Press.

______. 1977b. "Sacrifice and Social Structure among the Kuranko." *Africa* 47(1):41-49, 47(2):123-39.

Johnson, John W. 1980. "Yes, Virginia, There is an Epic." *Research in African Literature* 11(3):308-326.

Jones, Arthur M. 1934. "African Drumming." *Bantu Studies* 8:1-16.

______. 1943. *African Music.* Rhodes-Livingstone Museum, Occasional Paper 2.

______. 1957. "Drums Down the Centuries." *African Music* 1(4):4-10.

______. 1959. *Studies in African Music.* 2 vols. London: Oxford University Press.

______. 1978. Review of "Les mendzang des chanteurs de Yaoundé" by Pie-Claude Ngumu. *Review of Ethnology* 5(2-3):23-24.

Kapferer, Bruce. 1979. "Entertaining Demons: Comedy, Interaction and Meaning in a Sinhalese Healing Ritual." *Social Analysis* 1:108-152.

Keil, Charles. 1979. *Tiv Song.* Chicago: University of Chicago Press.

King, Anthony. 1960. "Employments of the 'Standard Pattern' in Yoruba Music." *African Music* 2(3):51-54.

Knight, Roderic. 1974. "Mandinka Drumming." *African Arts* 7:25-35.

______. 1982. "Manding/Fula Relations as Reflected in the Manding Song Repertoire." *African Music* 6(2):37-47.

Koetting, James. 1970. "Analysis and Notation of West African Drum Ensemble Music." *Selected Reports, Institute of Ethnomusicology, UCLA* 1(3):115-46.

Kopytoff, Igor. 1971. "Ancestors as Elders in Africa." *Africa* 41(2):129-42.

Krige, J. D., and E. J. Krige. 1954. "The Lovedu of the Transvaal." In *African Worlds: Studies in the Cosmological Ideas and Social Values of African Peoples,* edited by Daryll Forde, pp. 55-82. London: International African Institute/Oxford University Press.

Kubik, Gerhard. 1965. "Transcription of Mangwilo Xylophone Music from Film Strips." *African Music* 3(4):35-41.

______. 1972a. "Oral Notation of Some West and Central African Time-Line Patterns." *Review of Ethnology* 3(22):169-76.
______. 1972b. "Transcription of African Music from Silent Film: Theory and Methods." *African Music* 3(4):28-39.
______. 1983. "The Emics of African Musical Rhythm." Unpublished manuscript.
Kuhn, Thomas S. 1977. *The Essential Tension: Selected Studies in Scientific Tradition and Change*. Chicago: University of Chicago Press.

Laṣebikan, E. L. 1956. "The Tonal Structure of Yoruba Poetry." *Présence Africaine* N.S. 8/10.
Lawal, Babatunde. 1977. "The Living Dead: Art and Immortality among the Yoruba of Nigeria." *Africa* 47(1):50-60.
Leach, Edmund. 1961. "Two Essays Concerning the Symbolic Representation of Time." In *Rethinking Anthropology*, pp. 124-43. London: Athlone Press.
Lewis, J. David, and Andrew J. Weigert. 1981. "The Structures and Meanings of Social Time." *Social Forces* 60:432-62.
Little, Kenneth. 1954. "The Mende of Sierra Leone." In *African Worlds*, edited by Daryll Forde, pp.111-37. London: Oxford University Press.
Locke, David. 1978. "The Music of Atsiagbekọ." Ph.D. dissertation, Wesleyan University.
Lord, Albert B. 1960. *The Singer of Tales*. Cambridge: Harvard University Press.

Merriam, Alan P. 1973. "The Bala Musician." In *The Traditional Artist in African Societies*, edited by Warren L. d'Azevedo, pp. 23-81. Bloomington: Indiana University Press.
______. 1977. "Analysis of African Music Rhythm and Concepts of Time Reckoning." Paper Presented at the Society for Ethnomusicology Meeting. Austin, Texas, November 4.
______. 1982. "On Objections to Comparison in Ethnomusicology." In *Cross-cultural Perspectives on Music*, edited by Robert Falck and Timothy Rice, pp. 174-90. Toronto: University of Toronto Press.
Monts, Lester P. 1981. "Music and Regionalism in Liberia: The Vai Song Repertoire as an Indicator of Ethnic Interaction." Paper presented at the African Studies Meeting, Bloomington, Indiana, October 23.
Murphy, William P. 1976. "A Semantic and Logical Analysis of Kpelle Proverb Metaphors of Secrecy." Ph.D. dissertation, Stanford University.
______. 1980. "Secret Knowledge as Property and Power in Kpelle Society: Elders versus Youth." *Africa* 50:193-207.

Needham, Rodney. 1967. "Percussion and Transition." *Man* 2:606-614.
Nettl, Bruno. 1956. *Music in Primitive Culture*. Cambridge: Harvard University Press.
______. 1964. *Theory and Method in Ethnomusicology*. New York: Free Press.
Niangoran-Bouah, G. 1964. "Calendriers traditionnels et concept de temps." *Bulletin d'Information et de Liaison des Institutes Ethno-Sociologie et de Geographie Tropicale* (Abidjan) 1:9-26.
Nketia, J.H. Kwabena. 1955. *Funeral Dirges of the Akan People*. Achimota: University of Ghana.
______. 1958. "Traditional Music of the Ga People." *African Music* 2(1):21-27.
______. 1971. "History and Organization of Music in West Africa." In *Essays on Music and History in Africa*, edited by Klaus P. Wachsmann, pp. 3-25. Evanston: Northwestern University Press.
______. 1973. "The Musician in Akan Society." In *The Traditional Artist in African*

Societies, edited by Warren L. d'Azevedo, pp. 79-100. Bloomington: Indiana University Press.

______. 1974. *The Music of Africa*. New York: W. W. Norton.

Noss, Philip A. 1975. "The Ideophone: A Linguistic and Literary Device in Gbaya and Sango with Reference to Zande." In *Directions in Sudanese Linguistics and Folklore*, edited by Sayyid H. Hurreiz and Herman Bell. Khartoum: University of Khartoum.

Ogilby, John. 1670. *Africa*. London: Thomas Johnson.

Okara, Gabriel. 1964. *The Voice*. London: Heinemann.

Olney, James. 1972. *Metaphors of Self*. Princeton: Princeton University Press.

Ouologuem, Yambo. 1971. *Bound to Violence*. New York: Harcourt Brace Jovanovich.

Packard, Randall M. 1981. *Chiefship and Cosmology: An Historical Study of Political Competition*. Bloomington: Indiana University Press.

Paulme, Denise. 1940. *Organization sociale des Dogon (Soudan français)*. Paris: Éditions Domat-Montchrestien, F. Loviton.

Riesman, Paul. 1981. "African Contributions to Our Notions of Self, Society, and Human Relations" (Response to Wyatt MacGaffey's paper: "African Ideology and Belief, A Survey"). African Studies Meeting, Bloomington, Indiana, October 21-24.

Rigby, Peter. 1968. "Some Gogo Rituals of 'Purification': An Essay on Social and Moral Categories." In *Dialectic in Practical Religion*, edited by Edmund R. Leach, pp. 153-78. London: Cambridge University Press.

Rouget, Gilbert. 1971. "Court Songs and Traditional History in the Ancient Kingdoms of Porto-Novo and Abomey." In *Essays on Music and History in Africa*, edited by Klaus P. Wachsmann, pp. 27-64. Evanston: Northwestern University Press.

Rowell, Lewis. 1985. "Editorial: The Temporal Spectrum." *Music Theory Spectrum* 7:1-6.

Rycroft, David. 1977. "Evidence of Stylistic Unity in Zulu 'Town' Music." In *Essays for a Humanist: An Offering to Klaus Wachsmann*, pp. 216-60. New York: Town House Press.

Samarin, W. J. 1965. "Perspective on African Ideophones." *African Studies* 24:117-21.

Sapir, J. David. 1969. "Diola-Fogny Funeral Songs and the Native Critic." *African Language Review* 8:176-91.

Scheub, Harold. 1970. "The Techniques of the Expansible Image in Xhosa *Ntsomi* Performances." *Research in African Literatures* 1(2):119-46.

______. 1972. "The Art of Nongenile Mazithathu Zenani, A Gcaleka Ntsomi Performer." In *African Folklore*, edited by Richard M. Dorson, pp. 115-42. Garden City, New York: Anchor/Doubleday.

Schieffelin, Edward L. 1985. "Performance and the Cultural Construction of Reality." *American Ethnologist* 12:707-724.

Schutte, Gehard. 1980. "Social Time and Biological Life: The Case of a Venda Child's Burial." *Anthropos* 75:257-63.

Schutz, Alfred. 1971-73. *Collected Papers*. 3 vols. The Hague: Martinus Nijhoff. Vol. I, edited by Maurice Natanson, 1973; Vol. II, edited by Arvid Brodersen, 1971.

Seeger, Charles. 1951. "Systematic Musicology: Viewpoint, Orientations and Methods." *Journal of the American Musicological Society* 4(3):240-48.

Sempebwa, E. K. K. 1948. "Baganda Folk-Songs: A Rough Classification." *Uganda Journal* 12:16-24.

Serwadda, Moses, and Hewitt Pantaleoni. 1968. "A Possible Notation for African Dance Drumming." *African Music* 4(2):47-52.

Skarda, Christine A. 1979. "Alfred Schutz's Phenomenology of Music." *Journal of Musicological Research* 3:75-132.

Smith, Pierre. 1973. "Principes de la personne et catégories sociales." In *La notion de personne en Afrique noire,* Colloques Internationaux du C.N.R.S. No. 544, pp. 467-490. Paris: Editions du Centre National de la Recherche Scientifique.

Stone, Ruth M. 1975. Field Notes and Texts. Research Project in Bong County, Liberia.

______. 1979. "Communication and Interaction Processes in Music Events among the Kpelle of Liberia." Ph.D. dissertation, Indiana University.

______. 1982. *Let the Inside Be Sweet: The Interpretation of Music Event Among the Kpelle of Liberia*. Bloomington: Indiana University Press.

______. 1984. "The Power to Perform Without the Power to Know." Unpublished manuscript.

______. 1985. "In Search of Time in African Music." *Music Theory Spectrum* 7:139-48.

______. 1986. "Commentary: The Value of Local Ideas in Understanding West African Rhythm." *Ethnomusicology* 30:54-57.

Stone, Ruth M., and Verlon L. Stone. 1972. *Music of the Kpelle of Liberia.* New York: Folkways Record Corporation, FE4385.

______. 1981. "Event, Feedback and Analysis: Research Media in the Study of Music Events." *Ethnomusicology* 25:215-25.

Thompson, Robert Ferris. 1974. *African Art in Motion: Icon and Act*. Los Angeles: University of California Press.

______. 1983. *Flash of the Spirit*. New York: Random House.

Thornton, Robert. 1980. *Space, Time, and Culture Among the Iraqw of Tanzania*. New York: Academic Press.

Turner, Victor. 1967. *The Forest of Symbols: Aspects of Ndembu Ritual*. Ithaca: Cornell University Press.

Vansina, Jan. 1965. *Oral Tradition: A Study in Historical Methodology*. Translated by H. M. Wright. Chicago: Aldine.

Wachsmann, Klaus P. 1958. "A Century of Change in the Folk Music of an African Tribe." *International Folk Music Journal* 10:52-56.

Wagner, Gunter. 1954. "The Abalyyia of Kavirondo (Kenya)." In *African Worlds: Studies in the Cosmological Ideas and Social Values of African Peoples,* edited by Daryll Forde, pp. 27-54. London: Oxford University Press.

Waterman, Richard. 1952. "African Influences on the Music of the Americas." In *Acculturation in the Americas,* edited by Sol Tax. Chicago: University of Chicago Press, 2:207-18.

Zahan, Dominique. 1960. *Sociétés d'initiation bambara: Le n'domo, le korè*. The Hague: Mouton.

Zaslavsky, Claudia. 1973. *Africa Counts*. Westport, Conn.: Lawrence Hill.

Zemp, Hugo. 1967. *La Musique dan la vie*. (Liner notes.) Paris: OCORA.

______. 1971. *Musique Dan*. Paris: Mouton.

INDEX

www.ingramcontent.com/pod-product-compliance
Lightning Source LLC
LaVergne TN
LVHW040157080826
844660LV00001B/8

* 9 7 8 0 2 5 3 3 1 8 1 8 3 *